Savage, Allan G.
    An introduction to chess

AN INTRODUCTION TO CHESS

THE CREATIVE GAME

Allan G. Savage
National Master

A SPECTRUM BOOK

Prentice-Hall, Inc., Englewood Cliffs, N.J. 07632

Library of Congress Cataloging in Publication Data

Savage, Allan G.
    An introduction to chess, the creative game.

    "A Spectrum Book."
    Includes index.
    1. Chess. I. Title.
GV1446.S29   794.1'2   82-401
ISBN 0-13-479279-3   AACR2
ISBN 0-13-479261-0 (pbk.)

This Spectrum Book is available to businesses and organizations
at a special discount when ordered in large quantities.
For information, contact Prentice-Hall, Inc.,
General Publishing Division, Special Sales, Englewood Cliffs, N. J. 07632.

A SPECTRUM BOOK

10 9 8 7 6 5 4 3 2 1

Editorial/production supervision by Frank Moorman
Cover design by Honi Werner
Manufacturing buyer: Cathie Lenard

0-13-479279-3

0-13-479261-0 {PBK.}

PRENTICE-HALL INTERNATIONAL, INC., *London*
PRENTICE-HALL OF AUSTRALIA PTY. LIMITED, *Sydney*
PRENTICE-HALL CANADA INC., *Toronto*
PRENTICE-HALL OF INDIA PRIVATE LIMITED, *New Delhi*
PRENTICE-HALL OF JAPAN, INC., *Tokyo*
PRENTICE-HALL OF SOUTHEAST ASIA PTE. LTD., *Singapore*
WHITEHALL BOOKS LIMITED,, *Wellington, New Zealand*

CONTENTS

iii

FOREWORD

Since its origins, probably in India or Persia during the seventh century A.D., chess has amused, confused, astounded, confounded, attracted, and distracted countless enthusiasts throughout the civilized world. For most, it is a pleasant diversion, an escape from the pressures of reality. For others, it can be an ego-shattering, life-or-death struggle, a means of existence. Welcome to this strange and beautiful universe.

The human passion for chess has been well documented. The literature devoted to the game exceeds that of all other games combined. Benjamin Franklin, a skillfull chessplayer, wrote an essay entitled "The Morals of Chess," as valid today as it was in 1786. Concerning the value of the royal game to other disciplines, Franklin wrote:

> By playing at Chess, then, we may learn: First, Foresight...
> Secondly, Circumspection ... Thirdly, Caution ... and
> lastly, we learn by Chess the habit of not being discouraged by present bad appearances in the state of our affairs;
> the habit of hoping for a favorable chance, and that of
> persevering in the search of resources.

To learn what chess can teach you, you must first learn to play the game. As with any other recreational pursuit, the gratification you

v

derive from playing will increase in relation to the level of skill you attain. If you expect to play reasonably well and maintain a consistent rate of improvement, then a solid foundation, grounded in an understanding of chess basics, is absolutely essential.

My own chess background can serve as an illustration. I learned the moves and elementary principles at age eight from my father; although I immediately developed a passion for the game that is still very much alive today, my dad's lessons left me confused about the rules and fundamentals of sound play. For several years, victory eluded me, and I attributed my few successes to a judicious choice of opponent. The trend began to reverse itself after I joined my high school chess club and began to use its library. I then combined study with a regular routine of tournament practice and obtained a Master ranking while still in my teens.

Whatever your goal, your chess education must start with a good introductory manual, and *An Introduction to Chess: The Creative Game* is an important choice. National Master Allan G. Savage has channeled his considerable chess experience into this clearly written book and developed an approach unique in two respects. First is his use of the algebraic system of chess notation. The notation is used throughout the rest of the world, but has not been used in chess books published in the United States until recently. As of January 1981, however, algebraic notation is the only officially recognized notation accepted by F.I.D.E., the world governing body of chess.

The second unique aspect of this book's approach is the emphasis on the "elements" of chess. Most beginning books deal with the three stages of the game—opening, middle game, and endgame—but here you will study the main elements of sound chess and then see how they apply to the various stages. The approach is becoming popular among chess tutors, but Mr. Savage seems to be the first author to present it in a beginner's manual.

An Introduction to Chess will guide you through the tortuous road ahead and may stimulate your appetite for further chess study. Absorb the lessons, apply them to your games, and climb the chess ladder as high as you can. *Excelsior!*

JEFFREY M. KASTNER
Secretary, Manhattan Chess Club

PREFACE

This book has been written specifically for anyone afraid to play chess. For whatever reason, whether you feel the game is for intellectuals only or you have heard that it is far too complicated to learn, you have rejected the idea of playing chess.

Close your mind to what you have heard. The myths about chess and chessplayers are just that: myths. *Anyone* can learn to play, and anyone can enjoy chess regardless of his or her level of competence. The purpose of this book is to introduce you to a whole new universe of existence: the chessboard. The rules and elementary strategies are presented in a clear, straightforward fashion, enabling you to orient yourself in that new universe with little trouble. The book will not make you a master overnight, but it will give you enough knowledge and practical hints to enjoy playing at your own level and your own pace.

So relax! This will not be a heavy trip, but an exciting adventure. You are about to learn one of the greatest pastimes mankind has ever devised—a game played by paupers and kings alike. It is a game so simple that you will know enough in just a few short hours to give you a lifetime of pleasure, yet so rich that its mysteries will probably never be solved.

I wish to thank Symbols International for use of their Chessprint® transfers in preparation of the diagrams. I am also indebted to

W. Bradley Ryan, Esq. for his kind legal advice. Special thanks go to my many students, from whom I have learned much.

Finally, I am especially grateful to Donna Rothenberg for her aid in proofreading the manuscript and her unfailing support.

ALLAN SAVAGE

For my fifth grade teacher Mrs. Woolsey,
who gave me my first chess book.

I
THE RULES

chapter one
HOW THE
CHESS PIECES MOVE

On each turn, a player must move any one of his or her pieces and may capture an opponent's piece as a result. The pieces move in different ways, and no two pieces of the same color can occupy any given square at one time. No piece except the Knight can jump over another piece in its path. Thus the movement of the pieces is limited by the type of piece that moves as well as by the position of the other pieces on the board.

A player's move may also involve the **capture*** of an opponent's piece. Except for the Pawn, every piece captures in the same way that it moves; the capture is executed by removing the opponent's piece from the square it occupies and replacing it with the capturing piece. The captured piece is removed from the board and from further participation in the game.

The game is played on a board of 64 squares divided into eight rows of eight squares each. The vertical rows are called **files** and the horizontal rows are called **ranks.** Each player has sixteen pieces, eight of which are Pawns.

The King, the tallest **piece** on the board, moves one square at a time in any direction, horizontally, vertically, or diagonally. See Figure 1–1.

---

*Words in boldface are defined in the glossary.

3

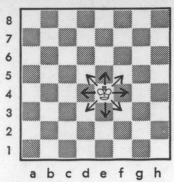

Figure 1-1 How the King moves.

The Rook, usually shaped like the tower of a castle, moves horizontally or vertically, any number of squares that it can travel without interference. See Figure 1-2. Since no two pieces of the same

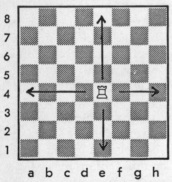

Figure 1-2 How the Rook moves.

Figure 1-3 Legal moves of the White Rook.

color may be on a single square simultaneously, White in Figure 1-3 may legally move the Rook to any square marked with an "x" or may capture the Black Pawn. White may not play to the squares marked with a black dot, since another piece interferes with that movement. To execute the capture of the Pawn, White removes the Black Pawn from the board and places the White Rook on the vacated square (Figure 1-4).

The Bishop, always topped with a bishop's miter, moves

Figure 1-4   The White Rook has captured the Black Pawn.

diagonally and may go as far as the player chooses, so long as there is no interference. As you can see in Figure 1-5, the Bishop travels only on squares of one color.

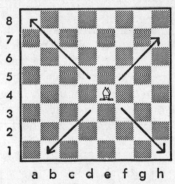

Figure 1-5   How the Bishop moves.

The Queen, the second tallest piece, combines the moves of the Rook and Bishop; it can move in any direction, horizontally, vertically, or diagonally, to any distance so long as the squares are open. See Figure 1-6.

The Knight, usually shaped like a horse's head, is the only piece that can jump over other pieces of either color. It moves in an L-shaped pattern, two squares in one direction and one square perpendicularly, as in Figure 1-7. Though it can jump over other

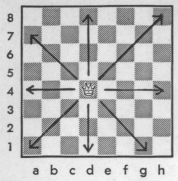

Figure 1-6   How the Queen moves.

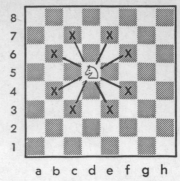

Figure 1-7   How the Knight moves.

pieces, it is prevented from moving to a square occupied by a piece of its own color.

Pawns move forward one square at a time, although on each Pawn's first move, the player has the option of moving two squares forward. But this option exists on the first move only. The Pawn is the only piece that captures in a different way than it moves. It is also the only piece that cannot move backwards. Pawns capture by advancing one square diagonally forward, after removing the captured piece from that square. Note that Pawns cannot *capture* an opponent's piece directly ahead of it and cannot *move* on the diagonal. This may be confusing at first, but it will become familiar with practice. Figure 1-8 illustrates how Pawns move, and Figure 1-9, how they

Figure 1-8   How the Pawn moves.

Figure 1-9   How the Pawn captures.

capture. The White Pawn on the left in Figure 1-9 may only capture the Black Pawn diagonally adjacent. It cannot move (or capture) forward. The White Pawn on the right has no legal move or capture.

chapter two
THE OBJECT
OF THE GAME

The object of a chess game is to capture the opponent's King, although unlike all other captures, the King is never actually removed from the board. When the King is attacked and has no legal place to move or no legal way to stop the attack, it is said to be **checkmated**, and the game ends (Figure 2-1). The player whose King is checkmated loses.

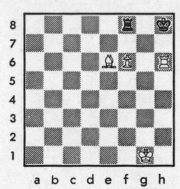

Figure 2-1   Black is checkmated.

At any time during the game when a King is attacked (threatened to be captured by an enemy unit), the King is said to be **in**

check (Figure 2-2). Upon attacking the opponent's King, it is customary, although not mandatory, for the attacker to say **"Check"** aloud. When your King is in check, you must get out of the position immediately. If any player fails to notice that he or she is in check and makes another move leaving the King still under attack, this fact must be pointed out and the illegal move retracted.

Figure 2-2   Black is in check by the White Knight.

There are three ways to get out of check: capturing the piece giving check, placing a piece between the attacker and the King, or moving the King itself. It is illegal for either King to move into check (to move to a square attacked by any enemy piece). This also means the two Kings may never be directly adjacent. In Figure 2-1, the Black King is checkmated because it cannot capture the White Rook which gives check; it cannot interpose a piece between the White Rook and Black King; and it has no legal move, because all immediately adjacent squares are guarded by the White Rook, Bishop, or Pawn.

A game may also result in a **draw**, with no winner or loser. There are a number of ways for this to occur, according to the rules of chess. All of these are listed below but the beginner is usually only concerned with the first three:

1. The players may agree to a draw at any time. This occurs when one player audibly offers "Draw?" and the other accepts.
2. If there is not sufficient material on the board for either side to give

checkmate, the game is drawn. For instance, if each player is left with only a King, the game is a hopeless draw. Other material situations that are inadequate for checkmate by either side will be covered later.

3. If a position arises where one side has no legal move, *but is not in check,* the game ends in a form of draw called **stalemate.** See Figure 2-3.

Figure 2-3   Black has been stalemated.

4. If any exact position is repeated three times during a game, though not necessarily consecutively, with the same person on the move each time, either player may claim a draw.

5. If either side can demonstrate that it can give check continuously, the game ends in **perpetual check.** This is a draw and quite different from checkmate.

6. If fifty moves by each side are played without any Pawns moving or anything being captured, either side may claim a draw. This is called the fifty-move rule. (The number of moves has been extended for certain rare special cases, but you needn't be concerned with these now.)

chapter three
SPECIAL MOVES

Castling

Castling is a special move in which the King and Rook combine their moves. It is the only time during the game when a player may move more than one piece on a single turn. Castling is shown in Figures 3-1 to 3-3. Each player may castle only once during a game. Castling may be undertaken on either side of the board when all of the squares between the King and the Rook on a particular side are vacant. The following conditions must exist for castling to be legal:

Figure 3-1   Piece placement before castling.

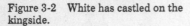

Figure 3-2 White has castled on the kingside.

Figure 3-3 White has castled on the queenside.

1. The King and Rook must be on their original squares, and neither may have been moved during the game up to that point.
2. The King cannot be in check.
3. The King cannot pass over a square attacked by an enemy piece.
4. The King cannot land on a square attacked by an enemy piece.

To castle, move the King two squares horizontally and move the Rook to the square next to and just past the King. The King should be touched and moved first, to satisfy the **touch move** rule (see Chapter 5).

Promotion

When a Pawn has traveled all the way down the board and reaches the last rank, it must be promoted. The Pawn is removed from the board and replaced with either a Queen, Rook, Bishop, or Knight of the same color. Since the Queen is the most valuable piece, it is most commonly chosen to replace the Pawn. In fact, **promotion** is often called **queening.** It does not matter if there are still like pieces on the board—a Pawn may be promoted to any of the four pieces mentioned. (See Figures 3-4 and 3-5.) Of course, a Pawn may both capture a piece and promote on the same move, as in Figure 3-6.

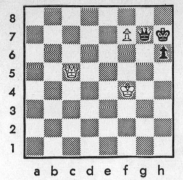

Figure 3-4 Position before promotion.

Figure 3-5 White has promoted the Pawn to a Queen.

Figure 3-6 White may capture the Bishop and promote simultaneously.

En passant

A special optional Pawn move exists whenever a Pawn of one color stands on its own fifth rank, and a Pawn of the opposing color stands on its original square on an adjacent file (Figure 3-7). If the opposing Pawn moves two squares from its original square, the advanced Pawn has the option of capturing it **en passant** (in passing) as if the opponent had moved only one square (Figures 3-8 and 3-9). This option only exists to the capturing Pawn *immediately*

Figure 3-7   The position before *en passant.*

Figure 3-8   Black has advanced his
Pawn two squares.

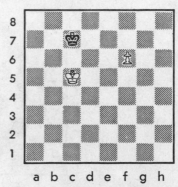

Figure 3-9   White has captured
en passant.

following the two-square advance. If the player fails to exercise this
option on the very next move, the right to capture *en passant* is
forfeited in that situation. However, capturing *en passant* may occur
many times during a game by either player in different areas of the
board.

chapter four
CHESS NOTATION

A convenient system of notation exists so that anyone can follow moves in a book or record the moves of a game quickly. This system, known as **algebraic notation,** is used throughout the world.

In Figure 4-1, you can see that each square on the board has one and only one name, derived from the grid of numbers and lower case letters as shown. The ranks are numbered from White's side of the board and the letters denoting the files start on White's left.

Pieces are designated by capital letters. Pawns have no specific designation but are referred to by the file on which they stand—

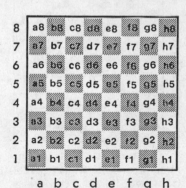

Figure 4-1   Algebraic notation.

"a-pawn", "b-pawn", and so on. The most commonly used symbols are:

K = King	0-0-0 = castles queenside
Q = Queen	e.p. = en passant
R = Rook	! = good move
B = Bishop	!! = very good move
N = Knight	? = dubious move
x = captures	?? = blunder
+ = check	− = to
0-0 = castles kingside	

To describe or record how a piece moves in notation, follow these simple steps by listing:

1. The symbol of the piece that moves (excluding Pawns)
2. The name of the square it was resting on before moving
3. The action it takes
4. The square the piece moves to.

For example, in Figure 4-2, White might move his e-pawn one square forward: e2-e3. Since Pawns have no designated symbol, the first step above is omitted when writing Pawn moves. The hyphen (-) indicates movement to a square.

Instead of the above move in Figure 4-2, White might capture

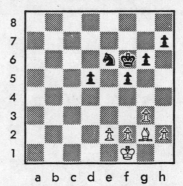

Figure 4-2 Write White's possible moves in notation.

Black's d-pawn with the move Bg2xd5; the capture is denoted by an "x."

Figure 4-3   The starting position.

Play over the game below in order to practice using the notation. Set up the board as in Figure 4-3.

1 e2-e4	c7-c5
2 Ng1-f3	Ng8-f6
3 Nb1-c3	d7-d5
4 e4xd5	Nf6xd5
5 Bf1-b5+	Bc8-d7

Figure 4-4   Position after Black's fifth move, 5 ... Bc8-d7.

Do you have the correct position (see Figure 4-4)? If not, start from the beginning of the game and try again.

6 Nf3-e5	Nd5xc3
7 Qd1-f3	f7-f6
8 Qf3-h5+	g7-g6
9 Ne5xg6	Ke8-f7
10 Ng6-e5+	Resigns

Figure 4-5   Final position where Black gave up.

chapter five
SETTING UP
THE BOARD AND PIECES

The board is always placed so that a White square is in the right-hand corner nearest you. The Rooks are placed in the corners. The Knights are placed next to the Rooks, and the Bishops placed next to the Knights. The Queen is placed "on her own color"; the White Queen is placed on the central white square on its own back row (d1) and the Black Queen on the central black square on its back row (d8). The Kings are placed on the remaining squares in the respective back rows (e1 and e8). Each side places its eight Pawns on the row directly in front of the pieces.

Figure 5-1   The starting position.

White always has the first move. Proper chess etiquette requires you to move a piece if you touch it, if it is legal to do so. Therefore, it is important to get into the habit of not touching a piece until you are absolutely sure what you are going to move. If you wish to adjust a piece on its square, you must first say aloud "I adjust" or **"J'adoube,"** making it clear that you are adjusting and not moving the piece. Following these rules may seem rather formal, but adherence to them helps avoid disputes and makes the game much more pleasant. Before a game begins, you should make sure your opponent knows this **touch move** rule. All experienced players automatically play with this rule understood.

chapter six
RELATIVE VALUE OF THE PIECES

As you will see, the numbers and kinds of forces each player has are almost always a crucial factor in determining who wins the game. It follows that, as you exchange and trade off pieces and Pawns for your opponent's forces, you want to get the best deal possible. In order to do this intelligently, you must be aware of the relative value of the pieces. For instance, it should be most obvious that a Queen is more valuable than a Bishop since the Queen has more ways to move than a Bishop. Likewise, a Bishop is more valuable than a Pawn. But how many Pawns is a Bishop worth, or how many pieces are equivalent to a Queen? The answers to these questions are very important for a good understanding of chess.

The relative value of the pieces are based on the Pawn being assigned the value of 1. On this scale, the Bishop and Knight are worth 3 each, the Rook 5, and the Queen 9. The Queen and Rooks are commonly referred to as the **major pieces,** and the Bishops and Knights are called the **minor pieces.** The term "pieces" usually refers to the major and minor pieces and not the Pawns.

In practice, it has been suggested that these values are not very exact, and in fact, may be significantly inaccurate, especially for the minor pieces. In top level play, the Bishop is ranked generally slightly better than the Knight, especially in endgames. Furthermore, in relation to the other pieces, the minor pieces are probably

21

worth more than 3 units. As you develop your chess ability, you might want to think of the Bishop as having a value of 3½ and the Knight 3¼. For the present, though, you can ignore these fractions and get along quite well.

This value system provides a basis for making sound exchanges. Here are some exchange situations that arise frequently in play. It should be obvious that the Queen, being the most valuable piece, should not be traded for any other single piece except the opponent's Queen. However, giving up your Queen for two Rooks is actually a good deal most of the time.

The Rook is approximately equal to a minor piece *plus* two Pawns. Therefore, trading your Rook for only a Bishop or Knight is usually a bad deal. This type of trade has a special name called "losing **the Exchange**" or "giving up the Exchange," that is, giving up your Rook for a minor piece.

Two minor pieces are worth more than a Rook. Often you might have the opportunity to give up two minor pieces for a Rook and Pawn. According to the table of values, this is an equal trade. However, more often than not, two pieces are more valuable than a Rook and Pawn. This is where the fractions, mentioned above, are useful. Therefore, you should be wary of this kind of trade.

Bishops and Knights are considered approximately equal, but the Bishop is slightly better more often than the reverse. It is important to understand their differences. The Bishop is a long-range piece, that is, it can travel from one part of the board to another very quickly. However, the Bishop can only control squares of one color and so can affect only half the board. The Knight is a short-range piece with its peculiar hop, but it can reach every square on the board. Consequently it is really the position of the other pieces and Pawns which determines whether a Bishop or Knight is better in any given position. If the position is somewhat open (say a number of Pawns have been exchanged), the Bishops may have free diagonals on which to operate and would be more powerful than the Knights. If the position is locked up (if the Pawns have no moves), the Knights are a bit better as they can jump, whereas the Bishops' diagonals may be blocked by Pawns.

Pawns have the lowest material value, but that does not mean they are worthless. The advantage of a single extra Pawn is sometimes enough to win endgames. Remember, Pawns can be promoted to new pieces if they reach the last rank. Three Pawns are considered approximately equal to a minor piece. This is important to remember as it is often possible and worthwhile to **sacrifice** a minor piece for two Pawns *plus* an attack on the King. The strength of such an attack is the crucial element here because, if it fails to produce checkmate or a further gain of material, you will have made a poor trade.

chapter seven
A SAMPLE GAME

In order to get further acquainted with chess notation and the way
the pieces move, play over the following sample game.

Hoffman-Petroff
(Warsaw, 1844)

1	e2-e4	e7-e5
2	Ng1-f3	Nb8-c6
3	Bf1-c4	Bf8-c5
4	c2-c3	Ng8-f6
5	d2-d4	e5xd4
6	e4-e5	Nf6-e4

Figure 7-1   After 6 . . . Nf6-e4.

24

The center is opening up, and the Kings have not castled. Such a situation is quite dangerous for both sides.

	7 Bc4-d5	Ne4xf2!
	8 Ke1xf2	d4xc3+
	9 Kf2-g3	....

Figure 7-2   After 9 Kf2-g3, White's King is in danger.

White had to get out of check at once. Black has given up a Knight, but has three Pawns for it, and has exposed White's King.

	9	c3xb2
	10 Bc1xb2	Nc6-e7
	11 Nf3-g5?	Ne7xd5
	12 Ng5xf7	....

Figure 7-3   Has Black been tricked?

If now 12 ... Ke8xf7 then 13 Qd1xd5+ and 14 Qd5xc5.

>   **12 ....**   **0-0!!**

Black sacrifices his Queen because he has calculated that the White King is fatally exposed. If White now plays 13 Qd1xd5, instead of capturing the Queen, then Rf8xf7 still leaves the White King in trouble. Therefore, White grabs the booty and hopes to weather the attack.

>   **13 Nf7xd8**   **Bc5-f2+**
>   **14 Kg3-h3**   **d7-d6+**

If White now answers the check with 15 g2-g4, then Nd5-f4 is checkmate.

>   **15 e5-e6**   **Nd5-f4+**
>   **16 Kh3-g4**   **Nf4xe6**

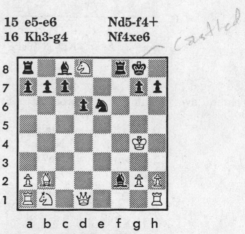

Figure 7-4   The White King is fatally exposed.

In spite of White's tremendous material advantage, he is lost because his King is too exposed. Black now threatens ... Rf8-f4+, which leads to mate.

17 g2-g3	Ne6-d4+
18 Ne8-e6	Bc8xe6+
19 Kg4-h4	Nd4-f5+
20 Kh4-h3	Nf5-e3+
21 Kh3-h4	Ne3-g2+
22 Kh4-h5	g7-g6+
23 Kh5-g5	Bf2-e3 mate

In check with no legal move, the White King is checkmated.

Figure 7-5 Checkmate!

II
THE ELEMENTS

chapter eight
MATERIAL

At the outset of a chess game, each side is given an equal number of forces (pieces and pawns) to use. Occasionally games arise where not all of one's forces are brought into action, but generally speaking, each unit has value and should be utilized. When one player retains more forces than the other, we say the former has a material advantage.

Perhaps the most important general principle in chess is that superior force usually wins. In the final stages of a game, a direct attack on the King in order to produce checkmate determines the outcome. However, most games are really decided by a number of tactical skirmishes or **combinations** that produce a material advantage. This advantage is then used to gain more material (such as promoting a Pawn to a Queen), ultimately forcing a decisive attack on the King.

It follows that it is vitally important for you to maintain your forces. If you must exchange, be careful not to get the raw end of the bargain: always be aware of the *value* of the pieces you are exchanging. (If you don't remember the values, review Chapter 6 and memorize them.) This is not to say that you need to be overly cautious and play passively. Though the smallest material advantage of one Pawn is often enough to win at the master level, your early games will rarely be decided in this manner. At this stage you should

31

be concerned with avoiding the loss of major pieces without obtaining **compensation.** There will be more to say on this point in later chapters.

Now let's examine the use of material advantages at various stages of the game. Although the distinction is not clear, the **opening** stage generally ends after both players have developed most of their pieces (about ten to twelve moves into the game), and the **endgame** begins when the Kings can walk around without fear. The **middle game,** usually the longest stage, lies in between. For an extended definition, see the glossary. Let's start with the endgame, where the final exploitation of a material advantage takes place.

THE ENDGAME

Large material advantages

When your material advantage is vastly superior and your winning should not be in doubt, there is only one pitfall that will concern you: *draw by stalemate.* This is one of the worst fates that can ever befall a chess player. Until you are able to avoid this problem without conscious effort, you must be constantly on your guard.

Try to understand the method behind the following examples of checkmating the King when a large material advantage exists. There are many ways to reach checkmate, but the method given is a systematic way to avoid the frustration of a careless stalemate.

Figure 8-1   Form a plan to confine the Black King.

King and Queen vs. King presents the easiest case. Examine Figure 8-1. First you should fix in your mind which side of the board you wish to drive the Black King towards. Let's say we have decided to drive it towards the a-file.

1 Qf1-d3   ....

The Black King is now confined to the rectangle in Figure 8-2. The plan is to make this rectangle smaller and smaller as the King is driven towards the a-file. Note that the process is conducted without checking the Black King and without using the White King. The method is to place the Queen a "Knight's jump" away from the Black King.

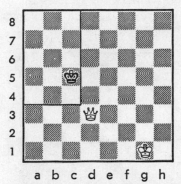

Figure 8-2   White has enclosed the Black King in the indicated area.

1	....	Kc5-c6
2	Qd3-d4	Kc6-c7
3	Qd4-d5	Kc7-b6
4	Qd5-c4	Kb6-b7
5	Qc4-c5	Kb7-b8
6	Qc5-c6	Kb8-a7
7	Qc6-b5	Ka7-a8

Now the most important rule: As soon as the Black King steps into a corner, *stop moving your Queen and bring up your King.* If you remember to *stop and think* as soon as the Black King reaches the corner, you cannot go wrong. On the other hand, if you continue to move a Knight's jump away, the move 8 Qb5-b6 produces stalemate. The rest plays itself.

8 Kg1-f2	Ka8-a7
9 Kf2-e3	Ka7-a8
10 Ke3-d4	Ka8-a7
11 Kd4-c5	Ka7-a8
12 Kc5-c6	Ka8-a7
13 Qb5-b7 mate	

With the King and Rook vs. King, the task is similar but slightly more involved as the White King must be used in the confining process. See Figure 8-3: White plays **1 Rb4-b5+**. This is the key position. White can drive back the Black King (in this case towards the eighth rank) by checking when the two Kings are opposing each other, one square apart.

Figure 8-3   Restriction with a Rook.

| 1 Rb4-b5+ | Ke5-f6 |
| 2 Ke3-e4 | .... |

Note that White does not play 2 Ke3-f4 (thus creating the opposing Kings position) as it is then *Black's move*. White needs to create that position with *White to move*. After the move played, 2 Ke3-e4, Black would lose ground by 2 ... Kf6-e6 since White then has 3 Rb5-b6+. So Black must retreat.

| 2 .... | Kf6-g6 |

If Black had played the King to the seventh rank, White would have responded 3 Rb5-b6.

3	Ke4-f4	Kg6-h6
4	Kf4-g4	Kh6-g6
5	Rb5-b6+	Kg6-f7
6	Kg4-g5	Kf7-e7
7	Kg5-f5	Ke7-d7
8	Kf5-e5	Kd7-c7
9	Rb6-h6	Kc7-d7

Now White must lose a move to continue the method.

Figure 8-4   White must waste a move.

10	Rh6-g6	Kd7-c7
11	Ke5-d5	Kc7-b7
12	Kd5-c5	Kb7-a7

White can now continue the method with 13 Kc5-b5 Ka7-b7, 14 Rg6-g7+, and so on, but has a quicker finish.

13	Rg6-g7+	Ka7-b8
14	Kc5-c6	Kb8-a8
15	Kc6-b6	Ka8-b8
16	Rg7-g8 mate	

The bigger your material advantage, the easier it is to checkmate. But you must be extra careful since it is also easier to stalemate. In this case it is best, when running down the opposing King, to use only one or two of your extra pieces and leave the others behind.

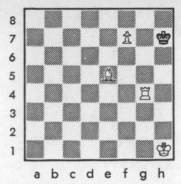

Figure 8-5 Embarrassment of riches.

For instance, in Figure 8-5 if White in his greed plays 1 f7-f8(Q), thus promoting the Pawn, Black is stalemated.

With King and two Bishops vs. King, the final procedure is somewhat tricky, because White must use all three pieces. As a result, the stalemate possibilities increase considerably.

I will leave the confining process to the reader. From Figure 8-6 you can see that two Bishops placed next to each other create an impenetrable barrier to the opposing King. The goal, of course, is to make this area continuously smaller as you drive the King into the corner. With careful play from Figure 8-6, you should be able to reach Figure 8-7. The task is now to force the Black King into the corner. The final scheme is to reach b6 or c7 with the White King. Once the King reaches either of those key squares, the rest is easy.

Figure 8-6 Restriction with two Bishops.

Figure 8-7 Watch for stalemates!

1 Bd6-e5   . . . .

And not 1 Ke6-e7 stalemate.

1	. . . .	Kc8-d8
2	Ke6-d6	Kd8-c8
3	Be5-f6	Kc8-b8
4	Kd6-d7	Kb8-a7
5	Kd7-c7	Ka7-a6
6	Bf6-c3	Ka6-a7
7	Bc6-b5	Ka7-a8

Now all that remains is for White to lose a move.

8	Bc3-d2	Ka8-a7
9	Bd2-e3+	Ka7-a8
10	Bb5-c6 mate	

The case of Bishop and Knight and King vs. King is the most difficult. Again the procedure is to first drive the opposing King to the edge of the board and then into the corner. The problem is that mate can be forced only in the corner which contains the same color corner square as that on which the Bishop travels. An error in the confining procedure allows the opposing King to make a break for the "wrong" corner. Since the entire procedure takes about thirty moves from a random position, and errors add to this considerably, there is the danger of exceeding the fifty-move rule (see Chapter 2). This ending will not be presented in detail, as its rare occurrence and high degree of difficulty make its study impractical for the beginning student.

To complete this study of large material advantages, a list of certain material situations that are insufficient to force checkmate is given below. These situations presume that there are no Pawns present for either side.

Two Knights and King vs. King
Knight and King vs. King
Bishop and King vs. King
Rook and King vs. Bishop and King
Rook and King vs. Knight and King

This general rule holds for endings: If no Pawns remain on the board, one must be at least a Rook ahead in order to win.

Small material advantages

Now we come to the most fundamental ending of all: King and Pawn vs. King. An advantage of one Pawn is, of course, the smallest material advantage possible. Many complex endings eventually reduce to King and Pawn endings, so it is vitally important that you understand when such cases are wins and how to win them.

The key position is found in Figure 8-8. Regardless of who is on the move, White wins. Take special notice of the following: *The White King is on the 6th rank in front of the Pawn.* This position should be memorized. With White to move, play continues:

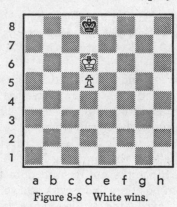

Figure 8-8   White wins.

1 Kd6-e6	Kd8-e8
2 d5-d6	Ke8-d8
3 d6-d7	Kd8-c7
4 Ke6-e7	....

And White successfully promotes the Pawn to a Queen and wins as in Figure 8-2. With Black to move, play in Figure 8-8 continues:

1	Kd8-e8
2 Kd6-c7	Ke8-e7
3 d5-d6+	White queens.

The question that arises in a practical game is whether or not the key position in Figure 8-8 can be achieved. If one's King cannot reach the sixth rank in front of the Pawn, the game is a draw (if defended correctly). Thus in Figure 8-9, play continues:

Figure 8-9   Black can draw.

1	Kd6-d7
2 Kd4-e5	Kd7-e7
3 d5-d6+	....

The Pawn reaches the sixth rank before the King, but there is no other way to make progress.

| 3 ...... | Ke7-d7 |
| 4 Ke5-d5 | Kd7-d8! |

The only move to draw the game.

5 Kd5-e6	Kd8-e8
6 d6-d7+	Ke8-d8
7 Ke6-d6	stalemate

If you have studied these principles, you are ready to tackle Figure 8-10. It follows from the above discussion that the first step should be to advance the King, *not the Pawn*. Thus:

Figure 8-10   White to move wins.

1 Kd1-e2   Kd8-d7
2 Ke2-d3!   Kd7-d6
3 Kd3-d4   . . . .

Black must now give ground. (Note that if it was White to move in Figure 8-11, the winning move would be d2-d3!, again forcing the Black King to give ground.)

Figure 8-11   Black to move.

3 . . . .   Kd6-e6
4 Kd4-c5   Ke6-d7

On 4 . . . Ke6-e5 White plays 5 d2-d4 + Ke5-e6, 6 Kc5-c6!, keeping the king *ahead* of the Pawn.

5 Kc5-d5! ....

And not 5 d2-d4 Kd7-c7!, and Black draws. You should work this out on your own.

5	Kd7-c7
6 Kd5-e6	Kc7-c6

On 6 ... Kc7-d8, 7 Ke6-d6! followed by advancing the Pawn leads directly to Figure 8-8.

7 d2-d4	Kc6-c7
8 d4-d5	Kc7-d8!
9 Ke6-d6!	....

Only this move wins. We have now reached the key winning position of Figure 8-8.

Finally it is important to mention that the winning outcome of Figure 8-8 does not apply if the Pawn is on the a or h files, as in Figure 8-12: after **1 Kh6-g6 Kh8-g8 2 h5-h6 Kg8-h8, 3 h6-h7** is a draw by stalemate.

Figure 8-12   The exception.

The decoy principle

In positions where you have a material advantage, the general rule is that your material is used to gain more material. For example, let's say that you have two pieces and your opponent only one, with many Pawns on both sides. You can use your two pieces to attack something, for instance, a Pawn, and your opponent can only defend it with one piece. Thus you will win the Pawn and acquire a *greater* material advantage.

When your material advantage is small, you must work harder to find a way to achieve a decisive superiority. Often this is accomplished in the endgame, by the use of a decoy.

From the previous examples, it should be apparent that, in Figure 8-13, White cannot possibly Queen the b-pawn if Black

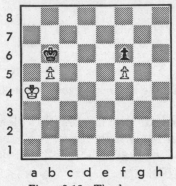

a b c d e f g h

Figure 8-13   The decoy.

defends accurately. It follows that the only way to win is on the other side of the board. White's extra Pawn is used to occupy the Black King while the decisive material *and positional* superiority is achieved elsewhere. This leads to the following general principle:

> In endgames with a minimal material advantage, it is often necessary to have play available on both sides of the board in order to force a win.

In Figure 8-13, play continues as follows:

1	Ka4-b4	Kb6-b7
2	Kb4-c5	Kb7-c7
3	Kc5-d5!	Kc7-b6

On 3 ... Kc7-d7, 4 b5-b6 wins.

4 Kd5-e6	Kb6xb5
5 Ke6xf6	Kb5-c6
6 Kf6-e7	White queens.

THE MIDDLE GAME

If you are fortunate enough to have a material advantage in the middle game, your goal should be to nurse this advantage into the endgame (or to trade it for some other strategic advantage—see Chapter 10). Striving for equal exchanges of major and minor pieces (but not too many Pawns) is one way to achieve this. The ultimate goal is, of course, a *simplified* endgame where your material advantage becomes decisive. If too many Pawns are exchanged, so that none at all remain, or that only a few remain on *one side of the board*, winning the game is much more difficult, if at all possible. This should be clear from the above endgame discussions. Remember that even if you are a minor piece ahead, but have no Pawns left, the result will usually be no more than a draw.

If you are playing a middle game with a material *disadvantage*, your goals should be to avoid massive trading of pieces (thus avoiding the endgame) and to try to create tactical complications (see Chapter 9).

In sum, the following general principle applies to the late middle game and early endgame:

If you are ahead in material, trade pieces but not Pawns.
If you are behind in material, trade Pawns but not pieces.

Be aware that I am referring to equal value trades: Bishops for Bishops, Rooks for Rooks, and so forth. It is usually not possible to avoid exchanging some pieces and Pawns, but do avoid wholesale mindless trading and simplification.

Another general rule that will help you is that a material advantage in the middle game is advantageous only if you can find some way to use your extra material. It does you no good to have an extra piece sitting on one side of the board if you are getting mated on the other. So remember to consolidate your position (that is, make use of all of your pieces) after you obtain a material advantage. Some examples are in order.

In Figure 8-14, Black has a large material advantage since he is the Exchange and one Pawn ahead. His plan should consist of using his extra material, hindering any of White's attacking chances, and slowly improving his position by offering to trade pieces.

Figure 8-14   Hillery-Savage (Boston, 1976).

22	Qc5-b4!
23 Qd2-f2	Ra8-e8

Black has centralized his pieces and intends to continue with Be6-d7-c6, offering trades and ultimately controlling the e-file with a Rook. White tries to get some counterplay by exposing Black's King, but the cost is a liquidation of many pieces. This is just what Black wants.

24 f4-f5	Be6xf5
25 Be4xf5	Re8xe1+
26 Nf3xe1	g6xf5
27 Qf2xf5	Qb4-c5!

Black now activates his pieces by offering to trade into an endgame. White must refuse as the more pieces traded, the closer Black gets to realizing his material advantage.

28	Qf5-f3	Qc5-d4
29	Bh4-f2	Qd4-f6
30	Qf3-g3	Qf6-c5!
21	Qg3-f3	Rf8-e8

Note how Black has centralized his Queen by offering trades. The last move finally activates the Rook and secures control of the e-file. Never forget to find a use for all of your pieces.

32	Ne1-d3	Qe5-e4
33	Qf3-d1	Re8-e6
34	Bf2-e1	b7-b6
35	Be1-f2	Re6-h6

And Black won.

In Figure 8-15, Black has a big advantage in material and position. The correct procedure would be to exchange pieces and then use the extra material to win more material. The following two continuations will emphasize the right and wrong way for Black to play this position.

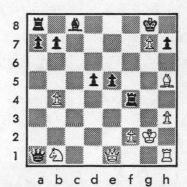

Figure 8-15   Exploitation of material advantage.

1	Nb1-d2	Qa1-d4
2	Nd2-f3	Qd4-e4!

Black correctly offers to trade Queens. If White declines, then Black's Queen will remain in an excellent central position.

3 Qe1xe4   d5xe4

3 . . . Rf4xe4 would be better to keep the Rook more active. Now, however, White cannot play 4 Nf3xe5, because after Rf4-f5 (forking two pieces), 5 Bh5-f7+ Rf5xf7, 6 Ne5xf7 Kg7xf7, White remains behind one piece *with no counterplay.*

4 Nf3-d2   Kg8xg7

This is not bad, but the g-pawn will not run away. Better is 4 . . . Bc8-e6, followed by developing the Rook on a8. Only then will Black be able to exploit his material advantage.

5 Rh1-c1   e4-e3!

This is very good, because it activates Black's Rook on f4.

6 f2xe3   Rf4xb4
7 Nd2-f3   b7-b5?!

Defense of the e-pawn is correctly ignored, since Black must activate his pieces, but better is 7 . . . Bc8-e6, developing the Bishop at once, with the Rook to follow.

8 Nf3xe5   Bc8-b7+
9 Kg2-g3   . . . .

Of course, not 9 Bh5-f3 Bb7xf3+, since trading pieces favors the player with the material advantage. White's only hope is to make something of his own active pieces before Black consolidates. White now threatens Rc1-c7+.

9 . . . .   Kg7-h6!
10 Bh5-e2   . . . .

Not 10 Bh5-g4, in order to reserve that square for the Knight.

| | 10 . . . . | Rb4-e4?? |

If Black plays 10 . . . Ra8-c8, thus neutralizing the activity of White's Rook and finally developing his last piece, he should have no trouble winning. Instead, Black gets greedy and leaves his material advantage idling on a8.

11	Ne5-g4+	Kh6-g5
12	Rc1-c5+	Kg5-g6
13	Be2-d3	. . . .

And White recovers his material deficit.

Now let's look at the way Black should have handled Figure 8-15.

1	Nb1-d2	Qa1xe1
2	Rh1xe1	e5-e4
3	Re1-c1	. . . .

White tries to activate his Rook on the open c-file.

| 3 | . . . . | Bc8-e6 |
| 4 | Rc1-c7 | Ra8-c8! |

Black is only concerned with activating his pieces. Defending the b-pawn with 4. . . Ra8-b8 would have been very passive. Now White must allow Black's second Rook to become active as trading on c8 would leave White with no counterplay to compensate for his large material deficit.

| 5 | Rc7-e7 | Rc8-c2! |

This is even better than 5 . . . Be6-f7, when White can temporarily prevent the invasion of his second rank with 6 Bh5-d1. After the text, trading pieces with 6 Re7xe6 Rc2xd2 is hopeless for White, since f2 falls anyway.

| 6 | Nd2-b3 | Rc2xf2+ |
| 7 | Kg2-g3 | Be6-f7 |

White resigns since he must trade Bishops (8 Bh5xf7+) or lose more material; for example, if 8 Bh5-d1 h7-h5! (threatening . . . h5-h4 mate!), 9 h3-h4 Rf4-f3+! wins two minor pieces for a Rook, leaving White a full piece down after 10 Bd1xf3 Rf2xf3+, 11 Kg3-g2 Rf3xb3.

Note how sound developing moves win faster than going for a quick kill once a material advantage is obtained, by comparing these last two examples.

THE OPENING

The prime consideration in the opening is the **development** of the pieces. Yet even here, you must not forget about conserving material. Though loss of material at this stage is rarely an immediate problem, the deficits will tell in the long run.

Opening gambits

Often one player may willingly give up material in the opening stage in return for other advantages, usually a gain in development (**time**). Such a sacrifice is termed a **gambit**. The struggle of material versus time is a classical opening battle. Most gambits invest a Pawn for the gain of one or two moves (**tempi**) in development. Such a lead in development must then be converted into other advantages, usually an attack, or the gambiteer will have no compensation for the material lost. A few examples are in order.

> *King's Gambit*
> 1 e2-e4   e7-e5
> 2 f2-f4   e5xf4

White's idea in this gambit is manifold. First, Black expends a tempo capturing the Pawn. The Black Pawn is deflected from the center, which White later hopes to control by an eventual d2-d4. Finally, White hopes to utilize the half-open f-file for an attack on the Black King. One variation continues:

> 3 Ng1-f3   g7-g5

4	Bf1-c4	g5-g4
5	0-0	g4xf3
6	Qd1xf3	....

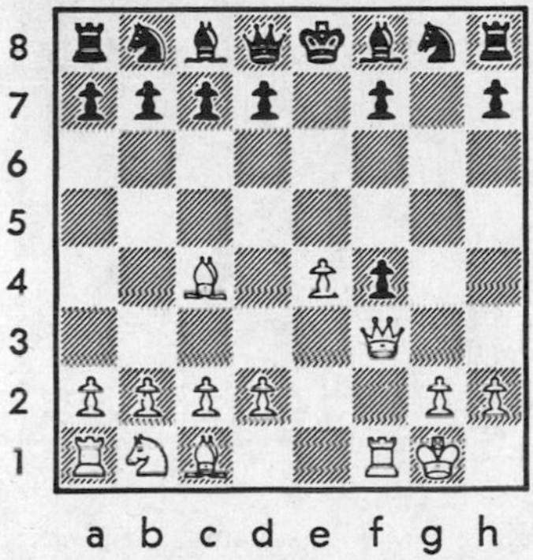

Figure 8-16   The Muzio Gambit.

White's plan in this position should be clear. He has further sacrificed a Knight, gaining many more tempi in development while Black captured the material. White has three pieces developed to Black's none. Furthermore, White has a very quick attack down the f-file after he captures the Black Pawn at f4, with f7 as a prime target.

But White's investment of a Knight is very serious. This is a very large material deficit, unusual for an opening gambit, which would be enough to lose the game if the attack fails.

Remember: Do not give away material unless you obtain good compensation.

Whether or not the compensation obtained for sacrificed material is adequate, is something that must be learned through trial and error. I encourage you to try playing and defending against gambits in order to become more familiar with the important relationship between material and time. Another example:

Danish Gambit

1	e2-e4	e7-e5
2	d2-d4	e5xd4
3	c2-c3	d4xc3

	4 Bf1-c4	c3xb2
	5 Bc1xb2	....

a b c d e f g h

Figure 8-17   The Danish Gambit.

Once again we see White give up material (two Pawns) to get a lead in development and fine attacking diagonals for his Bishops. Again note the quick focus on the target at f7. The f2 and f7 squares are the two most vulnerable squares in the opening since they are only defended by the King, a poor defender. Therefore, they are prime targets for early attacks.

Generally speaking, in the opening it is bad policy to play for the win of a small amount of material (Pawn) at the expense of development. Likewise, you should not try too hard to hold onto Pawns gambited by your opponent; it is better to give back the material to catch up in development. This will be clearer after playing over the following examples.

Queen's Gambit

1 d2-d4	d7-d5
2 c2-c4	d5xc4
3 Ng1-f3	Ng8-f6

If Black plays 3 ... b7-b5, there follows 4 e2-e3 c7-c6 (on 4 ... a7-a6, 5 a2-a4 Bc8-b7, 6 b2-b3! maintains White's advantage), 5 a2-a4 Qd8-b6 (on 5 ... a7-a6, 6 a4xb5 c6xb5, 7 b2-b3! Bc8-e6, 8 b3xc4 b5xc4, 9 Qd1-a4+ regains the Pawn with a better position—White is better developed and has better control of the center), 6 a4xb5 c6xb5, 7 b2-b3! c4xb3, 8 Qb1xb3 b5-b4, 9 Qb3-d5 Bc8-b7, 10 Bf1-b5+ Nb8-c6, 11 Nf3-e5. See Figure 8-18. This position strongly points out the difference in the development of the two **kingsides**. White is attacking both c6 and f7 and is therefore winning.

Figure 8-18   Position after 11 Nf3-e5 (analysis).

Note the move b2-b3 in the above variations. This removes the Black advanced c-pawn and opens lines favorably for White.

4	e2-e3	Bc8-g4
5	Bf1xc4	e7-e6
6	Nb1-c3	Nb8-d7
7	0-0	Bf8-d6

Examine Black's moves very carefully. See how he ignored the defense of the gambit Pawn in favor of sound developing moves.

Center Counter Defense

1	e2-e4	d7-d5
2	e4xd5	Ng8-f6
3	c2-c4	c7-c6
4	d2-d4	....

If White plays 4 d5xc6, Nb8xc6 leaves Black with superior development in compensation for the Pawn. With 4 d2-d4, White chooses to catch up in development while Black spends a tempo recovering the Pawn.

4	c6xd5
5 Nb1-c3	e7-e6

Figure 8-19   A gambit declined.

King's Gambit

1 e2-e4	e7-e5
2 f2-f4	e5xf4
3 Ng1-f3	d7-d5!

With this move, Black returns the gambit Pawn in a different way: he offers a Pawn to break up the White center. As we know, this is part of *White's* idea when playing 2 f2-f4 in the King's Gambit. The battle for central control is always of major importance.

4 e4xd5	Ng8-f6

Of course, Black does not play 4 ... Qd8xd5, since this loses a tempo to the developing move 5 Nb1-c3.

5 Bf1-b5+	c7-c6

This is better than 5 ... Bc8-d7, 6 Bb5-c4 when White's Pawn on d5 exerts strong pressure. Again, it is wise to try to exchange off your opponent's advanced Pawns.

6 d5xc6	b7xc6
7 Bb5-c4	Nf6-d5

| 8 d2-d4 | Bf8-d6 |
| 9 0-0 | 0-0 |

Black's advanced f-pawn gives him good chances of a kingside attack.

In conclusion, opening gambits may be accepted, but remain acutely aware of what you are giving up for the material gained. If it is development, often it is wise to return the extra material to recover the lost time. Holding on to the material is sometimes acceptable provided you can cope with your opponent's compensation.

Localized material advantage

Obtaining a material advantage in one sector of the board in the opening does not occur too frequently, but is more often seen in the middle game. It results from either faulty gambit acceptance, grabbing Pawns at the expense of development, or failing to watch the whole board. A localized material advantage is simply a preponderance of forces in one sector of the board. Such a position is ripe for triggering an attack and indeed *requires* you to attack. If you miss your chance, your opponent can consolidate the weakened sector by bringing up reinforcements and neutralizing the advantage. Take the position in Figure 8-20.

Black has gambited a Pawn to achieve a big lead in development. The Black Bishop on a6 prevents White from castling. (Remember, the King cannot pass over a square controlled by an enemy

Figure 8-20 Anderson-Savage (Boston, 1980).

piece.) The net result is that Black is ready to undertake middle
game operations while White is still playing the opening. White tries
to castle quickly, usually a good move, but here this only worsens the
problem and allows Black to achieve a localized material advantage
on the kingside.

1	Ne5-d3	Qe8-g6
2	0-0	....

Notice the lack of White pieces on the kingside.

2	....	Bd6xh2+!

This removes the King's only defenders—the Pawns. If now 3 Kg1xh2
Nf6-g4+ 4 Kh2-g1 Qg6-h5 5 Rf1-e1 Qh5-h2+ 6 Kg1-f1 Rf8xf2 mate.

3	Kg1-h1	Bh2-d6

White resigned. There is no good defense to 4 ... Nf6-g4, followed
by 5 ... Qg6-h5. If 4 f2-f3, Bd6-g3 and mate on h2 follows quickly.

As was said in the last section, you must be very careful after
accepting gambits. Following such an acceptance, use every opportunity to exchange off pieces so that your opponent has less force to
attack with. This point is brought home by the following vivid
example.

Kunin-Ochsenhuat
(Moscow, 1958)

1	e2-e4	e7-e6
2	d2-d4	d7-d5
3	Nb1-c3	Bf8-b4
4	Bc1-d2	d5xe4
5	Qd1-g4	Qd8xd4
6	0-0-0	f7-f5

Figure 8-21   Black is behind development.

While Black has spent time capturing two Pawns, White has con-
tinued his development and castled. Watch now as White produces
an attack by finding ways to develop his remaining forces without
losing time.

7 Bd2-g5	Qd4-e5??

Correct was 7 . . . f5xg4, 8 Rd1xd4 Bb4-e7!, trading off some of
White's active pieces, even though White will regain both Pawns
after 9 Bg5xe7 Ng8xe7, 10 Rd4xe4. Instead, Black avoids exchanges,
and the better developed White pieces lead to a decisive, localized
material advantage around the Black King.

8 Rd1-d8+	Ke8-f7
9 Ng1-f3!	Qe5-a5
10 Bf1-b5!	....

The threat of 11 Nf3-e5 mate is renewed, and 11 Bb5-e8+ is also
threatened. Black falters, but after the better 10 . . . g7-g6 (giving the
King a flight square), White plays 11 Qg4-f4, and his vastly superior
development should decide the game in his favor.

10	Nb8-c6
11 Nf3-e5+	Resigns

On 12 ... Nc6xe5, 13 Bb5-e8+ Kf7-f8, 14 Be8-h5 mate. Black never got his pieces developed.

Localized material advantages are more frequent when one side fails to castle early enough. However, on occasion, a player may castle too early directly into a preponderance of forces. Such examples serve as a strong warning against what is known as "castling into it."

Blom-Jensen
(Odense, 1934)

1 e2-e4	e7-e6
2 d2-d4	d7-d5
3 Nb1-c3	d5xe4
4 Nc3xe4	Bf8-d6
5 Bf1-d3	Ng8-e7
6 Bc1-g5	0-0?

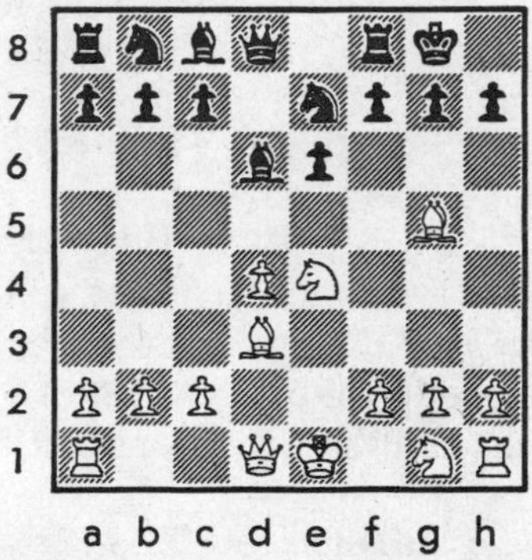

Figure 8-22   A case of "castling into it."

The tip-off here is the inadequate protection of the h7 square. A more normal castled position would have a Knight on f6, protecting against attacks on h7. White can bring up a great deal of material quickly into this sector.

7 Ne4-f6+!   g7xf6

If 7 ... Kg8-h8, 8 Qd1-h5 h7-h6, 9 Bg5xh6 g7xf6, 10 Bh6-g5+ Kg8-g7, 11 Qh5-h7 mate.

8 Bg5xf6   Qd8-d7

This was played in order to answer 9 Qd1-g4+ with Ne7-g6 without exposing the Queen to capture.

9 Bd3xh7+!   Resigns

It's mate after 9 ... Kg8xh7, 10 Qd1-h5+ Kh7-g8, 11 Qh5-h8.

Mieses-Amateur
Simultaneous Exhibition (Liverpool, 1900)

1 e2-e4	e7-e5
2 Nb1-c3	Ng8-f6
3 Bf1-c4	Nf6xe4
4 Qd1-h5	Ne4-d6
5 Bc4-b3	Bf8-e7
6 d2-d3	0-0?

Correct was 6 ... Nb8-c6, 7 Ng1-f3 g7-g6. In the game, Black's awkwardly placed Knight on d6 cannot aid the vulnerable h7 square. This Knight also blocks the d-pawn, preventing normal development of Black's queenside. The result: White can build up a localized material advantage on the kingside.

7 Ng1-f3	Nb8-c6
8 Nf3-g5	h7-h6

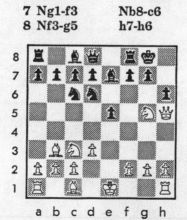

Figure 8-23   How can White bring up more attacking units?

This was forced since, if Black played 8 ... Be7xg5, 9 Bc1xg5 Qd8-e8, 10 Nc3-d5 has the winning threats of 11 Nd5xc7 and 11 Nd5-f6+! (11 ... g7xf6 12 Bg5xf6 leads to mate.)

9 h2-h4!   ....

This indirectly defends the Knight for, if Black now plays 9 ... h6xg5, 10 h4xg5, and White mates on h8 with the aid of the Rook. So Black tries to drive away the White Queen by returning the Knight to f6, but it is too late.

9		**Nd6-e8**
10 Nc3-d5		**Ne8-f6**
11 Qh5-g6!!		**Resigns**

Figure 8-24   After 13 Qh5-g6!! Black resigned.

White threatens Nd5xf6+ followed by Qg6-h7 mate. If 11 ... h6xg5, 12 Nd5xf6+ Be7xf6, 13 h4xg5 Rf8-e8, 14 Qg6xf7 mate. Finally, if Black takes the Queen with 11 ... f7xg6, there follows 12 Nd5xe7+ Kg8-h8, 13 Ne7xg6 mate!

chapter nine
TACTICS

INTRODUCTION

Tactics can be defined as the means used to carry out a strategy. They are represented by actual moves that use one or several of the following basic elements:

> pins
> forks
> overworked pieces
> checks
> discovered attacks

Examples of some of these have already been shown in the previous chapter. For instance in the game Blom-Jensen, of Figure 8-22, the pin of Black's Knight on e7 was important in White's combination. In Mieses-Amateur (Figure 8-24), the discovered attack by the Bishop on b3 and the pin of the f-pawn by the same Bishop prove fatal for Black in several variations.

Pins
The **pin** is perhaps the most commonly seen tactic in chess. We can find many examples of pins in every game from beginner to

grandmaster. A pinned piece is one which has lost its mobility because, if it were to move, greater losses would ensue. There are two major types: In Figure 9-1, you can see an example of a relative pin of Black's Knight on f6 by White's Bishop on g5. It is a relative pin because the Knight is pinned to a piece of relatively greater value—if the Knight were to move, Black's Queen would be captured by White's Bishop. A relative pin is usually sufficient to hinder mobility of the pinned piece, but you must be very careful that a material sacrifice is not possible. In Figure 9-1, it appears that White can take advantage of the pinned Knight and win a Pawn by 1 c4xd5 e6xd5, 2 Nc3xd5, but Black then plays the startling 2 . . . Nf6xd5!, 3 Bg5xd8 Bf8-b4+, and White finds a piece lost after. 4 Qd1-d2 Bb4xd2+, 5 Ke1xd2 Ke8xd8.

Figure 9-1   A relative pin.

In Figure 9-2, White's Knight on c3 is pinned to the King. Since it is illegal to move into check, White couldn't move the Knight if he wanted to. Any time a piece is pinned to the King, this is called an absolute pin. If White were to play 1 e4xd5, Black could play Qd8xd5 with no fear of losing the Queen.

The value of a pin is that it ties up the opponent's forces. The way to take advantage of this situation is to continue to attack the pinned piece with as much material as possible. When a piece of yours is pinned, the way to defend it is to try to break the pin as soon as possible.

Figure 9-2 An absolute pin.

Forks

A **fork** occurs when two units are attacked simultaneously. One of the most devastating tactics in chess, it alone is the most common cause of defeat for the beginner or novice. This occurs for two major reasons: (1) the novice is not very familiar with the powers of the pieces (how they move and capture), and (2) the novice does not pay sufficient attention to the entire board.

The first of these reasons can be corrected only by practice—the more you play, the more you will become familiar with the powers of each piece. Practice and experience are also helpful for the second problem, but a concentrated effort should be made during each game to continually survey the entire board. Only then will you be able to spot potential forks for both you and your opponent.

The most common forks occur with the Bishops and Knights. Figure 9-3 is a well known position from the Ruy Lopez opening. Black is a Pawn ahead, but is behind in development, and the center is opening up. The correct move is 1 . . . d7-d5 to protect the undefended Knight on e4 and return the Pawn. A grave mistake would be 1 . . . d7-d6, defending the e-pawn, because White would then have the move 2 Bb3-d5, forking Black's Knights and winning one of them.

Knight forks are often more difficult to see for the novice, since the Knight moves in a peculiar manner. A most embarrassing Knight

Figure 9-3   A potential fork.

fork of the King and Rook is known even to most beginners (Figure 9-4), but building on this simple idea requires some ingenuity. For instance, in Figure 9-5, Black can win a Pawn by being familiar with the above theme:

Figure 9-4   Common Knight fork.   Figure 9-5   Hidden Knight fork.

	1	Qd8xd4!
	2 Qd1xd4	Nb4-c2+
	3 Ke1-d1	Nc2xd4

The reason that this and other similar Knight forks are difficult to anticipate is that the two pieces to be forked are not yet located on the desired squares. In Figure 9-5, the White Queen had to be lured to d4 for the fork to take place. Let's take another example (Figure 9-6).

Figure 9-6 White can win a piece.

White can win at once if he is alert to a potential Knight fork:

1	Qc3-h8+!!	Kg8xh8
2	Ng5xf7+	and White wins

Queens, Rooks, Pawns, and even Kings also have the ability to fork two pieces. Practice is the best way to become familiar with situations in which forks are possible. A few easy practice problems follow. In each case, the player to move has a decisive fork available. Solutions can be found at the end of the chapter on page 123.

Figure 9-7 White to move.

Figure 9-8 White to move.

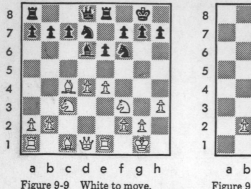

Figure 9-9   White to move.

Figure 9-10   White to move.

Overworked pieces

Very often in a chess game, certain pieces will be found to be burdened with too many tasks. Such pieces will be defending more than one piece or guarding too many vital squares. In these situations, you may be able to exploit the **overworked piece** with tactics, but you must first learn to recognize such a piece. Several examples of increasing difficulty follow.

In Figure 9-11, White can exploit the situation by recognizing that the Black Queen is overworked—it has the task of defending both Black Rooks. But how does White get the Black Queen to move?

Figure 9-11   The Black Queen is overworked.

1 Re5-e8+!!   ....

It turns out that the Black Rook on c8 is also overworked. Thus if
1 ... Rc8xe8 2 Qa1xc3.

1	Kh8-g7
2 Re8xc8	Resigns

After 2 ... Qc3xc8 4 Qa1xd4+ wins a Rook.

In Figure 9-12, White can exploit the fact that the Black Bishop
is overburdened with both the defense of the Pawn on h7 and the
control of a8. Thus White wins by:

Figure 9-12   The Black Bishop is overworked.

1 Bg8xh7!	Be4-b7
2 Bh7-g6	....

And White wins by promoting the h-pawn to a Queen.

Those examples were fairly simple. Now let's move on to more
complicated situations. In Figure 9-13, the White King is under
siege. Notice how Black's Bishops sweep down the strong diagonals
converging in the area of the White King. In such situations (with
very active pieces), you should look for ways to exploit your advantage by tactics. There is an overworked White piece in Figure 9-
13, but at this point it is quite hidden. Black must find a way to
further expose White's King and plays:

Figure 9-13   Converging attack.

1	Nf6-g4+
2 f3xg4	Qe7-f6+
3 Kf2-g1	....

White's other possible moves also lost: 3Kf2-e1 Qf6-e5, 4 Nc3-d1 Rd4xd1+!, or 3 Kf2-g3 Qf6-e5+, 4 Kg3-f2 Bh6xe3+, 5 Qc1xe3 Rd4-f4+, winning the Queen. After the text,* the White Queen is overworked. Why? What should Black play to take advantage of the situation?

3	Rd4-d1+!!

White resigns. If 4 Qc1xd1, Bh6xe3 mate; if 4 Nc3xd1, Qf6-f1 mate. The White Queen could not guard both e3 and f1.

　　Figure 9-14 is from the very famous game Adams-Torre (New Orleans, 1924). The setting looks quiet enough, but note that Black's King has no "air" and thus has what is called a weakness of the back rank. White is tactically alert and spots the weakness. This, together with the fact that a few of Black's pieces are overworked, produces a spectacular finale.

1 Qd4-g4!	Qd7-b5

*"Text" means the move actually played in the quoted game.

Figure 9-14   A grand finale.

Black's move is forced, because he must rescue his Queen, but he
cannot capture White's Queen, since this would lead to mate in two
moves (1 ... Qd7xg4, 2 Re2xe8+ Rc8xe8, 3 Re1xc8 mate).

2 Qg4-c4   Qb5-d7

Because of the mate, Black still could not capture the Queen with his
Queen or Rook, but what if he had played 2 ... Re8xe2? Then he is
still mated, this time by 3 Qc4xc8+ Qb5-e8, 4 Qc8xe8+ Re2xe8,
5 Re1xe8. Therefore, Black's move was again forced, but no damage
has been done. What does White have now?

Figure 9-15   Position after 5 Re2-e4!!
The Black Queen has no shelter!

	3 Qc4-c7!!	Qd7-b5
	4 a2-a4	Qb5xa4
	5 Re2-e4!!	....

The crowning blow! All of Black's major pieces are overworked, and
nothing of White's can be taken. You should work out the variations
for yourself. Meanwhile, the Black Queen is still under attack.

	5	Qa4-b5
	6 Qc7xb7	**Resigns**

There are no longer any retreats, so Black's Queen is lost.

Checks

There is a saying among chess players that has great merit:
"Always check, it may be mate." For the novice this is certainly
excellent advice. Since the object of the game is to corner the
opponent's King, attacking it directly by checking is often the first
step in achieving this goal. Very often a player can win material by a
check that is also a double attack, such as the Knight fork seen in
Figure 9-4.

In the opening, however, checks as a rule produce little advantage and may even lose time. The reason is that they can be easily
parried, since there is usually one or more pieces that can be inter-
posed. The following simple examples should convince you of this.

After the opening moves 1 d2-d4 d7-d5, 2 e2-e3 Ng8-f6, the
move 3 Bf1-b5+ is pointless, even though it appears to develop a
piece with a gain of time. Not only does Black have no less than five
ways to safely parry the check (Nb8-c6, Nb8-d7, Nf6-d7, Bc8-d7, and
c7-c6, the last two being the best), after Bc8-d7, 4 Bb5xd7+? (better
is 4 Bb5-d3) Nb8xd7 White is far behind in development and the
check has only helped Black.

Again from the opening position, after the moves 1 e2-e4 e7-e5
2 f2-f4 Qd8-h4+, White has only one adequate move (3 g2-g3), but it
renders the Queen check pointless.

Contrast this example with the variation 1 e2-e4 e7-e5, 2 f2-f4
e5xf4, 3 Nb1-c3 Qd8-h4+. Here White must play 4 Ke1-e2, since the
alternative 4 g2-g3 f4xg3, 5 Ng1-f3 g3-g2+!, 6 Nf3xh4 g2xh1(Q)
leaves White a Rook down.

Figure 9-16 Who is really better?

After 4 Ke1-e2 (Figure 9-16), White's King is certainly compromised, but he will be compensated by a strong center. Believe it or not, this rather peculiar opening position is known to theory. A sample continuation runs 5 . . . d7-d6, 6 Ng1-f3 Bc8-g4, 7 Nc3-d5 Ng8-a6 (stopping the fork), 8 Qd1-e1 Qh4-d8 (note the loss of time involved in 3 . . . Qd8-h4+), 9 Ke2-f2 Bg4xf3, 10 g2xf3 Na6-c5, 11 d2-d4 Nc5-e6, 12 c2-c3, and the position is considered unclear.

There are two types of checks that you should learn to look out for. One is called a **discovered check.** This occurs when a piece is moved which uncovers a check given by a second piece. Discovered check is the most powerful tactic in chess.

A very well known trap utilizing the discovered check occurs in the Petroff Defense after the opening moves 1 e2-e4 e7-e5, 2 Ng1-f3 Ng8-f6, 3 Nf3xe5 Nf6xe4? (3 . . . d7-d6 is correct), 4 Qd1-e2 Ne4-f6?? White now discovers a check with his Queen by moving the Knight to a devastating square 5 Ne5-c6+. Black must lose the Queen.

As can be seen, a discovered check is strong because the piece which exposes the check can do tremendous damage by either capturing material directly or moving to a threatening square—even if the material or the square is protected. This can be done with impunity, since it is the check to the King which must be met—not the possible threats by the discovery piece. An extreme example of this tactic is seen in Figure 9-17 in what is fondly known as the seesaw. Despite White's huge material deficit, he can win as follows:

Figure 9-17   The see-saw.

1	Rg7xf7+	Kh8-g8
2	Rf7-g7+	Kg8-h8
3	Rg7xe7+	Kh8-g8
4	Re7-g7+	Kg8-h8
5	Rg7xd7+	Kh8-g8
6	Rd7-g7+	Kg8-h8
7	Rg7xc7+	Kh8-g8
8	Rc7-g7+	Kg8-h8
9	Rg7xb7+	Kh8-g8
10	Rb7-g7+	Kg8-h8
11	Rg7xa7+	Kh8-g8
12	Ra7xa6 and wins.	

The other check that you must watch out for is the **double check.**
This is really a special case of the discovered check where the discovery piece also gives check. When a King is in check by two pieces
simultaneously, the only way to escape is to move away. Capturing
the checking piece or interposition is not possible. This is why the
double check is so powerful—either or both pieces giving check can
be **en prise.** A most well-known example is the **smothered mate.**
In Figure 9-18, White appears to be lost. Black's Queen can be won
by 1 Nf7-e5+ Ra8xa2, 2 Ne5xc6, but White remains hopelessly
behind in material. Yet White has a winning combination. The lesson
is that when you have a discovered check, examine *all* the possible
discoveries.

1 Nf7-h6++   ....

Figure 9-18   The famous smothered mate.

Note that neither the Knight nor the Queen can be captured since Black is in double check. And if Black replies 1 . . . Kg8-f8, then 2 Qa2-f7 is mate.

1	Kg8-h8
2 Qa2-g8+!!	Ra8xg8
3 Nh6-f7 mate	

This smothered mate is known as Philidor's Legacy, named after the famous 18th century French player François Philidor. Familiarity with this special tactic can pay off handsomely, as it does occur in many games. A similar idea can be seen in Figure 9-19. Though White has quite a few reasonable continuations in this position, only

Figure 9-19   Putting it all together.

one variation leads to a clear win. Notice the battery of the White Queen and Bishop on the same diagonal. Putting this together with your knowledge of discovered checks and Philidor's Legacy, can you come up with the winning variation?

> 1 Qf7-g8+!!   Kh8xg8
> 2 Nd5-e7++   Kg8-f8

Not 2 . . . Kg8-h8, 3 Ne5-f7 mate.

> 3 Ne5-g6+!!   h7xg6
> 4 Ne7xg6 mate

Perhaps the most famous example of the power of a double check occurred in a game between two top grandmasters of their day. The position in Figure 9-20 arose in Reti-Tartakower (Vienna, 1910). White won by:

Figure 9-20   A famous example.

> 1 Qd3-d8+!!   Ke8xd8
> 2 Bd2-g5++   Kd8-c7

On 2 . . . Kd8-e8, 3 Rd1-d8 mate.

> 3 Bg5-d8 mate

Discovered attacks

A more general example of the discovered check is the **discovered attack.** The idea is very similar—one piece moves and uncovers an attack by a second piece. The piece that moves also creates a threat and thus two threats are produced at once, both of which cannot be met. The following figures show two examples.

In the game Trifunovic-Aaron (Beverwijk, 1962), shown in Figure 9-21, White played **1 Bd5-g8!** and Black resigned since he cannot meet both threats of 2 Rd2xd8 and 2 Qf5-h7 mate.

Figure 9-21   Discovered attack!   Figure 9-22   Fancy footwork.

In Marshall-Rubinstein (Moscow, 1925) in Figure 9-22, White won by

1 Nf3-d2   Qb3-a2

The Black Queen must stay on the a2-g8 diagonal in order to guard the Bishop on f7 where an attack by the White Queen has been discovered.

2 Ne4-c3   Resigns

The Queen can no longer remain on the crucial diagonal.

Now that you have become somewhat familiar with elementary tactics, we shall examine how they are utilized in the different stages of the game.

THE OPENING

Opening traps

At this point, your impression of the opening is probably that it consists of a myriad of unfathomable variations that you will never be able to understand, much less learn to play. You should not worry about this. Even the top grandmasters do not know all of the openings. The important thing is that you understand basic opening principles, to be presented in the next chapter. If you carefully follow those principles and closely watch your tactics, you will be able to play the opening quite satisfactorily. Later, only after your tactical ability improves and your strategic knowledge deepens, should you undertake serious study of opening theory.

Perhaps the greatest fear of the novice is that of falling into a known opening trap. Occasionally, what may look like an obvious move turns out to be a subtle tactical trick. As already stated, the way to avoid such pitfalls is to develop according to recognized principles and stay tactically alert. A number of examples follow.

After the opening moves 1 e2-e4 e7-e6, 2 d2-d4 d7-d5, 3 e4-e5 c7-c5, 4 c2-c3 Nb8-c6, 5 Ng1-f3 Qd8-b6, 6 Bf1-d3 (Figure 9-23), you may think that White's last is an error since it blocks the White Queen's protection of the d-pawn. Black is attacking the d-pawn three times, White defending only twice. Do not get too alarmed— White is playing a gambit. Try to visualize the variation 6 . . . c5xd4, 7 c3xd4, Nc6xd4, 8 Nf3xd4 Qb6xd4. If you can't picture it in your

Figure 9-23   Can Black safely win a Pawn?

mind, play it out on the board. It turns out that Black has broken an important opening principle—he has gone Pawn-grabbing with the Queen in the opening. Ask yourself if White can take advantage of the situation after Black's eighth move. Sure enough, there is a devastating discovered check, 9 Bd3-b5+ followed by 10 Qd1xd4 winning the Queen. In this case, White's gambit was poisoned; Black should not grab the Pawn.

Figure 9-24 illustrates a different situation. This position arises from the popular Morra Gambit of the Sicilian Defense as follows: 1 e2-e4 c7-c5, 2 d2-d4 c5xd4, 3 c2-c3 d4xc3, 4 Nb1xc3 Nb8-c6, 5 Ng1-f3 d7-d6, 6 Bf1-c4 Ng8-f6? (correct is 6 . . . e7-e6). Black has underestimated the tactical possibilities of White's lead in development and plays what looks like a natural move. But White now answers 7 e4-e5!, giving Black some bad choices. For instance, 7 . . . Nc6xe5??, 8 Nf3xe5 d6xe5, 9 Bc4xf7+!, winning the Queen; or 7 . . . d6xe5, 8 Qd1xd8+ Nc6xd8 (worse is 8 . . . Ke8xd8, 9 Nf3-g5! Kd8-c7, 10 Ng5xf7 Rh8-g8, 11 Nc3-b5+ Kc7-b8, 12 Nf7xe5 and White is winning), 9 Nc3-b5 Ra8-b8, 10 Nf3xe5 e7-e6, 11 Nb5-c7+ Ke8-e7, 12 Bc1-e3 with a big advantage to White. Note the vulnerability of f7 and the very active White pieces in all of these lines.

Figure 9-24   White has a surprising shot.

Returning to Figure 9-24 after 7 e4-e5!, Black's lesser evil is . . . Nf6-g4, 8 e5-e6! Bc8xe6, 9 Bc4xe6 f7xe6, 10 Nf3-g5 Ng4-f6, 11 0-0! Qd8-d7, 12 Rf1-e1 e6-e5, 13 Qd1-b3, even though White has a clear advantage.

Another trap in the Morra Gambit is extremely vicious. After

1 e2-e4 c7-c5, 2 d2-d4 c5xd4, 3 c2-c3 d4xc3, 4 Nb1xc3 Nb8-c6, 5 Ng1-f3 d7-d6, 6 Bf1-c4 e7-e6, 7 0-0 Ng8-e7, 8 Bc1-g5 h7-h6? (Figure 9-25). Black mechanically tries to break the uncomfortable pin, but again falls victim to White's active pieces by 9 Nc3-b5!. Now 9 ... h6xg5 loses the Queen to 10 Nb5xd6+ Ke8-d7, 11 Nd6xf7+. So Black played (in Ney-Koblents, Tallin, 1956) 9 ... d6-d5, but after 10 e4xd5 h6xg5, 11 d5xe6! White had a winning attack.

Figure 9-25 White can exploit Black's poor development.

All of these examples show that you must be extremely careful when playing against an opening gambit with which you are unfamiliar. Routine moves are often faulty in such lines, so it is necessary to carefully examine each possible aggressive continuation. I recommend accepting most opening gambits, assuming they don't lead to an immediate loss, in order to become familiar with the relationship between material and time.

Attacking the uncastled King

Probably the most common opening mistake of beginners is failure to castle. In addition to avoiding this strategic error, it is very important for you to learn how to take advantage of the situation should your opponent decide to leave his or her King in the center.

The first step is the exposure of the King. It may be necessary for you to prevent castling by forcing the King to move or by controlling a square the King passes over. Figure 9-26 illustrates this idea. White has sacrificed two Pawns to obtain a tremendous lead in

Figure 9-26   White strands the Black
King in the center.

development and an open e-file. The first objective is to keep the
Black King in the center.

     10 Bc1-a3!   **d7-d5**

Not 10 ... Bc3xa1 11 Rf1-e1+ and White wins.

     11 Bc4-b5   **Bc3xa1**
     12 Rf1-e1+   **Bc8-e6**
     13 Qd1-a4   **Ra8-b8**
     14 Nf3-e5!   **. . . .**

Note the use of *all* the White pieces in the attack. Although he is a
Rook ahead, Black is helpless since his pieces cannot defend the key
sector.

     14 . . . .   **Qd8-c8**
     15 Bb5xc6+   **b7xc6**
     16 Qa4xc6+   **Ke8-d8**
     17 Ne5xf7+   **Be6xf7**
     18 Ba3-e7 mate.

Once the hostile King has been confined to the center, the next step
is to bring about its exposure by removing its defenders. Usually this
means destroying its Pawn protection. This creates open files and
diagonals—avenues of attack. Then the King must be drawn out into

the open. This stage often involves a sacrifice in order to facilitate exposure or to maintain the pace of the attack. In Figure 9-27, Black finds it impossible to castle kingside as 9 ... Ng8-e7 is met by 10 Nf3-g5 0-0, 11 Qd1-h5 with a double attack on f7 and h7. Therefore, it is necessary to try to limit the scope of the White pieces first. 9 ... Bc8-g4 is indicated, eventually exchanging off White's Knight on f3 if necessary. Instead, Black plays the passive 9 ... Bc8-d7?, probably intending ... Qd8-e7 and ... 0-0-0. White wastes no time opening lines before Black can get his King to safety.

Figure 9-27   Opening lines of attack.

9	Bc8-d7?
10 e4-e5!	d6xe5
11 Rf1-e1	Ng8-e7

It would probably be better to continue 11 ... Bd7-g4, although after 12 Qd1-b3! (12 d4-d5 Nc6-e7, 13 Re1xe5 opens the e-file but closes the a2-g8 diagonal), Black is still in big trouble.

12 Nf3-g5	Bd7-e6

Again, if 12 ... 0-0, 13 Qd1-h5. So Black is forced to return some material and allow his King to be exposed.

13 Bc4xe6	f7xe6
14 Ng5xe6	Qd8-d6
15 Ne6xg7+	Ke8-f8

Now that lines are open, White brings up more attacking units.

16	Qd1-g4	Bb6xd4
17	Nc3-e4!	Qd6-b4
18	Ng7-e6+	Kf8-e8
19	Ne4-f6+	Ke8-f7
20	Ne6-g5+	Kf7-f8

The Knight is taboo because 20 . . . Kf7xf6, 21 Qg4-e6+ leads to mate. But now both White's Rooks are threatened. White still has a winning combination based on the weak light squares in the Black position. First, though, he must stop . . . Qb4xe1 mate.

21	Bc1-a3!!	Qb4xa3
22	Qg4-e6	Nc6-d8
23	Qe6-f7+!!	Nd8xf7
24	Ng5-e6 mate	

A picturesque finish!

Figure 9-28   A unique checkmate.

Usually it is not so easy to mate once the opponent's King is exposed. A successful King hunt requires one to keep up the tempo of the attack while bringing in more reinforcements and, at the same time, preventing consolidation of the defense.

Figure 9-29 is taken from the game Tal-Gligoric (Zagreb, 1959). Since Black's kingside Pawns have moved, the only safe place

Figure 9-29   Black fails to castle.

for the Black King is on the queenside. Therefore, White quite
correctly begins his assault there.

         13 a2-a4!   **a7-a5**

Black decides he cannot allow a4-a5. But now Black's queenside has
been further weakened.

         14 Ra1-b1   **g5-g4?**

The object of this maneuver is to prevent Bd3-e4 from exploiting the
light-square weaknesses in Black's camp. But it would be better to
play 14 ... Qd8-e7, 15 Bd3-e4 0-0-0. White now finds a way to open
up the center and expose Black's monarch.

         15 Nf3-h4   **Nd7-f6**
         16 d4-d5!   **. . . .**

If Black now accepts the Pawn sacrifice with 16 ... e6xd5, White will
sink his Knight powerfully into f5, in addition to opening up the
center. If Black plays 16 ... e6-e5 (conceding f5, but trying to keep
the center closed), 17 c4-c5! with a subsequent Bd3-b5+ activates
White's forces.

         16 . . . .   **Qd8-e7**
         17 0-0   **Nf6-d7?**

Figure 9-30 Position after 17 0-0. Should
Black castle queenside?

Unfortunately, Black loses the Exchange if he castles queenside—
17 ... 0-0-0, 18 d5xe6 f7xe6 (Qe7xe6?? 19 Bd3-f5 wins), 19 Nh4-g6—
but he should have tried this, because, after 19 ... Qe7-g7, 20 Ng6xh8
Rd8xh8, Black has some attacking chances with ... h6-h5-h4. The
point is that at least the Black King is relatively safe in this line.

18 d5xe6		**Qe7xe6**

Now the Exchange sacrifice (f7xe6) makes no sense as White can
keep the Black King in the center with an eventual Bd3-g6+.

19 Bd3-f5		**Qe6xc4**
20 Rf1-d1!		**....**

Notice how White brings up all the pieces. Should Black now play
20 ... 0-0-0, then 21 Rd1-d4 Qc4-c5, 22 Rb1-b5 Qc5-a3, 23 Bf5xg4
leaves his game in ruins, but this was still the lesser evil. Now his
King is a sitting duck.

20		**Nd7-f6**
21 Rd1-d4		**Qc4-c6**
22 Bf5-e6!		**....**

Just look at the activity of White's pieces while Black's Rooks stand
as spectators. White now threatens Rd4-c4, trapping Black's Queen.

The Bishop is untouchable as 22 ... f7xe6, 23 Qc2-g6+ Ke8-d7,
24 Qg6-g7+ is curtains.

22 ....   Rh8-g8

Black is prepared to give up the Queen if White now plays 23 Rd4-c4
f7xe6 24 Rc4xc6 Bb7xc6, obtaining an approximate material equivalent (R+B+P). But White has better.

23 Be6-c4   Ke8-f8

Figure 9-31   White's initiative is beginning
to tell.

White threatened Bc4-b5. On 23 ... 0-0-0 24 Bc4xf7 or the stronger
24 Bc4-b5 Qc6-c5, 25 Nh4-f5 Kc8-b8, 26 Nf5-e7 Rg8-g5, 27 Rd4-c4
Qc5-e5, 28 Ne7-c6+ leaves White with a dominating position. Again,
note the maximum use of all of White's pieces in this last variation.
The White Knight on h4 is not left on the edge of the board, but is
brought into the thick of the fray. Replay this variation until you
appreciate the harmony of White's pieces.

24 Bc4-b5   Qc6-c5
25 Rd4-c4   Qc5-e5
26 Rc4xc7   ....

This is the first spoils of the weakened queenside. Black's army is in
total disarray, and the rest is just mopping up for a grandmaster. The

remaining moves were 26 ... Bb7-e4, 27 Bb5-d3 d6-d5, 28 Rc7-c6
Ra8-b8, 29 c3-c4! (the final destruction of the center) Rg8-g5, 30
c4-c5 d5-d4, 31 e3xd4 Qe5xd4, 32 Bd3xe4 Qd4xe4, 33 c5xb6 Qe4xc2,
34 Rc6xc2 and White won the ending with his extra Pawn.

    I would like to close this section with a final example of a King-
hunt gone wrong. This instructional example is included to demonstrate the final stage of an attack on the uncastled King: the con-
struction of a mating net and its attendant problems.

Tchigorin—Caro
(Vienna, 1898)

1 e2-e4	e7-c5
2 Nb1-c3	Ng8-f6
3 f2-f4	d7-d5
4 d2-d3	....

This move is far too passive and is the direct cause of White's
problems. 4 f4xe5 is correct.

4	Bf8-b4
5 f4xe5	Nf6xe4!
6 d3xe4	Qd8-h4+
7 Ke1-e2	....

Unfortunately, this is forced, because 7 g2-g3 loses a Rook to
Qh4xe4+.

7	Bb4xc3
8 b2xc3	Bc8-g4+
9 Ng1-f3	d5xe4

At first glance, it appears that the pin on the White Knight allows
Black to recover the piece easily. But appearances are deceiving as
White finds that pins are a double-edged weapon.

        10 Qd1-d4!   **Bg4-h5!**

Of course, if 10 ... e4xf3+, 11 g2xf3 leaves the Black Bishop pinned
to his Queen! So Black avoids that pin but finds that after 11 Ke2-e3!,

the e-pawn is still pinned and is now threatened with capture. Still, the complications are not over.

11	Ke2-e3	Bh5xf3
12	Bf1-b5+	....

If White had played 12 g2xf3, then Qh4-e1+, 13 Ke3-f4 Qe1-h4+ draws by perpetual check.

12	....	c7-c6
13	g2xf3	Qh4-h6+!

If instead 13 .. .... c6xb5, 14 Qd4xe4 Qh4xe4+, 15 Ke3xe4 leaves White with the better endgame due to his beautifully centralized King (see the endgame discussion in Chapter 10).

14	Ke3xe4!?	....

White makes a daring decision to play the middle game with an exposed King. After 14 Ke3-e2 Qh6-h3, 15 Rh1-d1 e4xf3+, 16 Ke2-f2 Qh3xh2+, the game is again drawn by perpetual check.

14	....	Qh6-g6+
15	Ke4-e3	c6xb5

Figure 9-32   A question of King safety.

Let's take stock of the situation in Figure 9-32. The material is even, and the White King is exposed in the center. If Black gets time to castle and bring his Rooks to the center files, the game is practically over. So White develops and strands the Black King in the center.

16 Bc1-a3!	Nb8-c6
17 Qd4-d5	Qg6xc2

This Pawn capture is quite playable, since White has no immediate threats and must attend to his exposed King. Black now threatens Qc2xc3+.

18 Ra1-c1	Qc2-f5

Now the White e-pawn is threatened, and 18 f3-f4 exposes the White King still further. So what is the answer? To find the right move, remember that the Black King is also exposed in the center.

19 Rh1-e1!   . . . .

Figure 9-33   What should Black play?

Both sides suffer from exposed Kings, but Black can solve his problems with one clever move. Can you find it?

19 ....   Ra8-d8?

Not 19 ... Qf5xe5+??, 20 Ke3-f2, and Black's opening of the central file is fatal to his Queen. The correct move was 19 ... b5-b4!, giving up a Pawn to castle. For if 20 Ba3xb4 Nc6xb4, 21 c3xb4 0-0, or 20 c3xb4 0-0, 21 b4-b5 Rf8-e8. In either case, it is the White King that suffers.

20 Qd5xb5   a7-a6
21 Qb5-b1   ....

The White Queen must guard d3, but on 21 Qb5-f1, Black plays ... Ke8-d7!!, followed by ... Kd7-c8 and ... Rh8-e8, "castling by hand" and connecting his Rooks. After the text 21 ... Ke8-d7 is impossible. Black now avoids exchanging Queens, as then the White King would not be in danger.

21 ....   Qf5-g5+
22 f3-f4   Qg5-g2
23 Ba3-d6   Qg2-h3+

Now Black must keep up the tempo of the attack. 23 ... Qg2xh2 would not do because White threatens 24 Qb1xb7.

24 Ke3-e4   f7-f5+
25 Ke4-d5   ....

Figure 9-34   The critical position.

This is the critical position of the game. The White King has been
hunted to and fro by judicious checks but has survived nevertheless.
There comes a time in all such attacks when the checking must stop
and the mating process begin. This is known as constructing a
mating net. Generally it is not done by checking directly, but by
cutting off the escape routes of the King.

In this game, Black now made the fatal error of giving useless
checks rather than constructing a net by restricting the escape
routes. The move leading to a probable win would have been
25 . . . Rd8-c8!! This hinders White's King's attempts to run away via
the c-file. The White King may now try to hide amongst Black's
Pawns or his own, or White might attempt a counterattack. Without
going through all the variations, I will give just a sketch of the possible lines after the correct 25 . . . Rd8-c8.

On 26 Kd5-c5 Qh3xh2, 27 Kc5-b6 Qh2xf4, 28 Kb6xb7 Qf4-c4!
wins.

On 26 Qb1xb7 Qh3-g2+, 27 Kd5-c5 Nc6-e7+, 28 Kc5-b6
Rc8-c6+, 29 Kb6-a7 Qg2-f2+, 30 Ka7-a8 0-0+, 31 Bd6-b8 Rc6-b6
wins.

Finally, White's best try is 26 Kd5-c4. Amazingly there is no
winning discovered check, yet White is extremely short of playable
moves while his King is caught in a crossfire. Black can play a solid
waiting move such as . . . g7-g6! and White is hard put to respond.
For example, if 27 Rc1-c2 b7-b5+, 28 Kc4-b3 Nc6-d4+; or if
27 Re1-d1 Qh3-e3! Best appears to be 27 Kc4-b3 but after Qh3xh2
with the further . . . Nc6-a5-c4, Black has a big edge.

Let us return to the game. You should carefully compare the
above lines with the game continuation, noting how it is often important to save your checks and hinder the King's escape *first.*

25	Qh3-g2+??
26 Kd5-c4	b7-b5+
27 Kc4-d3	Qg2-f3+
28 Kd3-c2	Qf3-f2+
29 Kc2-b3	Rd8-c8
30 Rc1-c2	Qf2xf4
31 Kb3-b2!	Nc6-a5
32 Kb2-a1!!	Qf4-c4?

The c4 square should be reserved for the Knight. Now White seizes the initiative and doesn't let up.

33	e5-e6	Na5-c6
34	Qb1-d1	h7-h5?
35	Re1-g1	Rh8-h7
36	Rg1xg7!	Resigns

On 36 ... Rh7xg7 37 Qd1xh5+ leads to mate.

THE MIDDLE GAME

Attacking the castled King

Tactics in the middle game most often involve an attack on the castled fortress. Before an examination of the methods involved, a discussion of the important aspects of the castled position is in order. (Reasons for castling are discussed in the opening section of Chapter 10.)

The major weakness of the castled position is that, for all practical purposes, the King's residence has been fixed. Since the King moves only one square at a time, vacating the castled position is a major undertaking and thus is carried out only when absolutely forced by a dangerous attack.

Given that the King's residence has been "advertised," it is only natural to retain some pieces and Pawns in the vicinity for its protection. Therefore, the general nature of the castled position is a passive one—a number of units must of necessity be immobilized for protection.

The major strength of the castled position is one that cannot be overemphasized:

In order to attack the castled King, the attacker must decentralize his or her pieces.

This is probably the single most neglected factor in all unsound attacks. The corollary to this is that one must have adequate control of the center before one begins an attack on the flank. The reason for this lies in the well known chess maxim:

An attack on the flank is best met by a counterattack in the center.

A defender of a flank attack who can break through and overrun the center with pieces and Pawns cuts the opponent's forces in two. Thus a central breakthrough will often steal the initiative from an inadequately prepared attack.

Enough of principles. Let's look at some appropriate examples. From Figure 9-35 play continues:

Figure 9-35   Geller-Euwe (Zurich, 1953).

12	Ne2-g3	c5xd4
13	c3xd4	Ra8-c8
14	f3-f4	Na5xc4
15	f4-f5	f7-f6
16	Rf1-f4	....

Black has reasonable control of the central squares, though his pieces appear cut off from the kingside. White's attack is based on the space advantage derived from his advanced Pawn on f5 (see the middle game discussion in Chapter 10). His last move plans the simple Rf4-h4 and Qd1-h5 with an unstoppable attack on h7. Yet Black does not panic and correctly sees that White's pieces will be seriously decentralized.

16 ....   b6-b5!

This excellent move further supports the Knight on c4 but, more importantly, opens b6 to activate the Black Queen.

17 Rf4-h4	Qd8-b6

The threat on the d-pawn must be met. Now it becomes clear that White's center is shaky, and he must make further concessions to get time for the h-file breakthrough.

18 e4-e5	Nc4xe5
19 f5xe6	Ne5xd3
20 Qd1xd3	....

20 e6xd7 fails to 20 ... Qb6-c6, threatening mate.

20	Qb6xe6
21 Qd3xh7+	Kg8-f7
22 Bc1-h6	....

Figure 9-36   White is seriously decentralized.

Yes, indeed, White has a strong attack, but his proud center has crumbled and his pieces are committed to the flank. Take careful note of Black's active Bishop, Queen's Rook, and Queen.

22	Rf8-h8!!

This forces the White Queen from the defense of c2—a further decentralization.

23 Qh7xh8	Rc8-c2

All of a sudden, White's King is more vulnerable and cannot be aided by his offside pieces. White now fails to find the best defense— 24 d4-d5 Bb7xd5 25 Ra1-d1 Rc2xg2+ 26 Kg1-f1 g7xh6 27 Qh8xh6, although Black would still have some winning chances due to the exposed White King.

24 Ra1-c1	Rc2xg2+
25 Kg1-f1	Qe6-b3
26 Kf1-e1	Qb3-f3

And White resigned.

Figure 9-37   Savage-Sarvis (Cambridge, Mass., 1980).

In Figure 9-37, Black has just played 22 ... Ra8-b8 with the intention of playing b5-b4 and sacrificing a piece to open the b-file. White also has a strong attack and only needs time to play h4-h5, opening up all the files on the Black King. Unfortunately, the immediate 23 h4-h5 is answered by h6xg5 and White must let his Knight on f6 hang if he is to keep the initiative, but the compensation is not clear. Instead, White makes a thematic central Pawn break, and Black, under time pressure, fails to see White's defensive idea.

23 e3-e4!	b5-b4?!

Black's best was probably 23 ... d5xe4 with some exchanges on e4, but then White has room to defend his King. After White's 23 e3-e4, Black was rightly afraid of e4-e5 supporting the Knight on f6, followed by h4-h5 and a breakthrough.

24 a3xb4	Na6xb4
25 c3xb4	Qe7xb4
26 g5xh6	Bg7xh6
27 Nf6-h5!	....

Black can capture neither Knight and must defend against the threat of Qf3-f6+. So ...

27	Rd8-d6
28 Qf3xf7	....

This was White's major point as it threatens 29 Rg1xg6, followed by 30 Rg6xh6+ and mate on g7. Black cannot play 28 ... g6xh5 as 29 e4-e5! is curtains. Yet Black can survive with 28 ... Bb7-c6!, 29 b2-b3 Rb8-b7! (missed by both players), and the White Queen must retreat, relinquishing several threats.

28	Bb7-a6?
29 b2-b3	c4xb3
30 Nd2xb3	Qb4-c3

Missing the defensive idea planned by White's 23rd move which cleared the third rank for the Rook.

31 Rg1-g3	Qc3-c4
32 Nh5-f6	Bh6-g7
33 Qf7xg6	Qc4-c7
34 Qg6-h7 mate	

Having looked at a few attacks that lacked central control, let's continue with some examples of correct attacking play. Prerequisites for an attack on the castled King include:

1. Control of the center, or a blocked or stabilized center.
2. Localized material advantage in the vicinity of the opposing King.
3. Open lines or the means of opening lines.

Alekhine—Lopez
(Almeria, 1945)

1	e2-e4	e7-e6
2	d2-d4	d7-d5
3	Nb1-d2	d5xe4
4	Nd2xe4	Nb8-d7
5	Ng1-f3	Ng8-f6
6	Bf1-d3	Bf8-e7
7	0-0	0-0
8	c2-c3	b7-b6
9	Qd1-e2	Bc8-b7
10	Rf1-d1	Rf8-e8

Without playing any spectacular moves, White has achieved a fine game, since Black failed to challenge White's central Pawn at d4 (by 6 ... c7-c5, for instance). Therefore, White has a small space advantage (see Chapter 10) and proceeds to occupy e5 as a prelude to a kingside attack.

11 Nf3-e5   h7-h6?

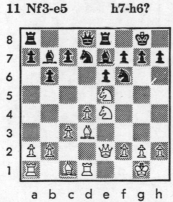

Figure 9-38   Position after 11 Nf3-e5.
Black should simply by exchanges.

Any Pawn moves in the castled position constitute a potential weakness. Black's last was uncalled for; he should have played 11 ...Nf6xe4, 12 Bd3xe4 Bb7xe4, 13 Qe2xe4 Nd7xe5, 14 Qe4xe5, exchanging off White's aggressively posted pieces. If you have a cramped position, it is usually wise to exchange.

12 Bc1-f4   Nf6-d5

Now it would be wrong to play 12...Nf6xe4, 13 Bd3xe4 Bb7xe4, 14 Qe2xe4 Nd7xe5?, because after 15 d4xe5, White's Pawn at e5 guarantees a clear advantage (see next section). Still, exchanging a few pieces is best, and Black should play the line above with 14...Nd7-f6.

13 Bf4-g3   Qd8-c8
14 Qe2-h5   ....

White now systematically masses his pieces on the kingside, obtaining a localized material advantage in that sector.

14 ....   Re8-f8
15 Ne5-g4   ....

Figure 9-39   White is ready to sacrifice.

White takes aim at Black's h6, threatening an unstoppable sacrifice to open lines. However, the real focal point is h7.

15 ....   f7-f5

There is nothing to be done. If 15 ... Nd7-f6, 16 Ng4xh6+ g7xh6,
17 Ne4xf6+ Nd5xf6, 18 Qh5xh6 (threatening Bg3-e5, Be5xf6 and
mate on h7) Nf6-e4, 19 Bg3-e5 f7-f6, 20 Qh6-g6+ Kg8-h8, 21
Be5-f4, recovering the Knight and coming out two Pawns ahead.

16 Ng4xh6	g7xh6
17 Qh5-g6+	Kg8-h8
18 Qg6xh6+	Kh8-g8
19 Qh6xe6+	Kg8-h8
20 Qe6-h6+	Kh8-g8
21 Qh6-g6+	Kg8-h8
22 Bg3-e5+	Nd7xe5
23 d4xe5	Qc8-e8

On 23 ... f5xe4, 24 Bd3xe4, and again h7 is the fatal focus.

24 Qg6-h6+	Kh8-g8
25 Ne4-g5	Be7xg5
26 Qh6xg5+	Kg8-h8
27 Bd3xf5	....

Now the only answer to the threats on h7 is 27 ... Rf8xf5, but after
28 Qg5xf5, White has a Rook and four Pawns for a Bishop and
Knight and a winning position. Instead Black preferred:

27	Qe8-f7
28 Qg5-h6+	Kh8-g8
29 Bf5-e6	Nd5-e7
30 Rd1-d3	Resigns

In Figure 9-40, White has a reasonably solid position vs.
Black's aggressive, but slightly weakened, formation (Black's castled
position has been somewhat weakened by the advance of the f-pawn).

11 Qd1-b3	Kg8-h8
12 Qb3xb7?	....

Correct was 12 Nd2-f1 to complete his queenside development.
Instead, White loses valuable time grabbing a Pawn and Black uti-
lizes the opportunity to build up a localized material advantage on

Figure 9-40   Gunsberg-Weiss (New York, 1889).

the kingside. Notice that Black is quite secure in the center and is therefore justified in his flank attack.

>   12 ....   Rf8-f6
>   13 Qb7-b3   Ra8-b8
>   14 Qb3-c2   Rf6-g6

White's characteristic central thrust to counter a flank attack, c3-c4, is impossible due to ... Nc6-b4 or even ... Ne4xd2, with the Pawn on d4 or the Knight of f3 loose after a series of exchanges. So White must wait for the onslaught.

>   15 b2-b3   Be7-d6
>   16 Bd3-e2   ....

White prepares to play 17 Nd2-f1, but never gets the chance. Black has systematically utilized almost all his forces, and now there only remains the line opening phase. First a weakness is forced.

>   16 ....   Bg4-h3
>   17 Be2-f1   Qd8-f6

Figure 9-41   White must weaken his castled position.

Black threatens 18 . . . Rg6xg2+, 19 Bf1xg2 Qf6-g6, 20 Nf3-h4 Qg6-g4, 21 Nd2-f3 g7-g5, with a winning attack. Therefore White is forced to weaken his Pawn formation and create a target for line opening.

18	g2-g3	Bh3xf1
19	Kg1xf1	Rb8-f8!

Black brings up his last piece and threatens 20 . . . f5-f4 opening up all the avenues of attack. Take special notice of how White's Pawn at g3 is used as a target for the file-opening f5-f4 advance. White's reply is desperation.

20	Nd2xe4	f5xe4
21	Nf3-h4	Rg6xg3!!
22	h2xg3	Bd6xg3

Now if 23 Nh4-g2, Bg3xf2 ends it all, as a devastating discovered check follows.

23	Kf1-g2	Bg3xh4
24	Bc1-e3	Qf6-f3+
25	Kg2-h2	Bh4-e7
26	Kh2-g1	Rf8-f6
27	Kg1-f1	Qf3-g4
28	Qc2-d1	Rf6-f3
29	Ra1-c1	Qg4-h3+

White resigned as he is mated after either 30 Kf1-e2 Rf3xe3+,
31 f2xe3 Qh3-g2, or 30 Kf1-g1 Rf3-f6, followed by ... Rf6-g6+.

Figure 9-42   Stahlberg-Menchik (Lodz,
1938).

Carefully examine the position in Figure 9-42. White is better
developed and has all of his pieces actively placed. The center is
under good control because of White's d-pawn. Thus conditions are
ripe for an attack on the Black King. All that is necessary is to loosen
up the castled position and secure a localized material advantage in
that sector. Play continues:

> **16 Nf3-g5   Qd6-f4?**

Black must develop. Best is 16 ... Bc8-d7, but not 16 ... h7-h6
17 Ng5xf7! Rf8xf7, 18 Qc2-g6 Qd6-f8, 19 Rc3-f3! with a winning
attack.

> **17 Ng5xf7!   Rf8xf7**
> **18 Rc3-f3   Qf4-c7**

Inadequate was 18 ... Qf4-d6, 19 Qc2-b3 Qd6-c7, 20 Bc4xf7+
Qc7xf7, 21 Re1-e8+, and so on.

> **19 Rf3-e3!   ....**

White is now threatening 20 Re3-e8+ as well as 20 Re3-e7.

19	Kg8-f8
20 Qc2xh7!	Bc8-g4

This development comes too late, but of course Black cannot play 20 ... Nf6xh7 because 21 Re3-e8 mate.

20 Qh7-h8+	Nf6-g8
21 h2-h3!	....

White forces the use of his f3 for the final frontal assault.

21	Bg4-f5
22 Bc4xf7	Kf8xf7
23 Re3-f3	Resigns

There is no defense to 24 g2-g4; for instance, if 23 ... Kf7-g6, 24 g2-g4 Bf5-d7, 25 Qh8-h5 mate.

Notice how White made use of all of his pieces. Black's queen-side Rook and Bishop were virtually bystanders while White obtained a localized material advantage in the vicinity of the Black King.

Use of Pawns in attacking

Your own Pawns can be used in many ways when attacking the castled King. When advanced directly, they can drive away defensive units and force weaknesses in the castled position. By exchanging them for your opponent's Pawns, you can open up lines of attack (files and diagonals) for your other pieces. If your own King is tucked away on the opposite side of the board, you can storm your opponent en masse by advancing an entire wing of Pawns. Last but not least, certain middle game attacks culminate in Pawn promotion, as the direct outcome of a victorious assault. Figure 9-43 is a good example of how Pawns are used in an attack.

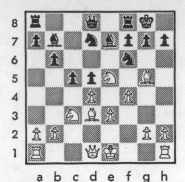

Figure 9-43   Black wrongly ignores White's attack.

11 0-0   c5-c4?

It should be clear that White is massing his pieces for a kingside assault. Therefore, Black should not relinquish the pressure on the center with 11 ... c5-c4, because his counterplay is now restricted. His best plan is to try to exchange off White's aggressively placed pieces. To that end, 11 ... Nf6-e4 would have been appropriate.

   12 Bd3-c2   a7-a6
   13 Qd1-f3   b6-b5
   14 Qf3-h3   g7-g6

White's last two moves have forced a breach in Black's castled position as a result of the threat of 15 Ne5xd7, 16 Bg5xf6, and 17 Qh3xh7 mate. Now White can use his f-pawn to force open a file for activation of his Rooks.

   15 f4-f5   b5-b4
   16 f5xg6   h7xg6
   17 Qh3-h4!   ....

White begins to exploit the weakness on f6 created by Black's 14 ... g7-g6. He willingly trades his Knight on c3 for Black's on f6, as this increases his material preponderance in the vicinity of the Black King. Also, this is logical as the Knight on c3 did not contribute to White's attack.

17	b4xc3
18 Ne5xd7	Qd8xd7
19 Rf1xf6!	....

White captures on f6 with his Rook, thus serving two purposes:
(1) He reserves his dark-squared Bishop to exploit the weakened
dark squares around Black's King. (2) He prepares doubling Rooks
on the newly opened f-file, thus bringing up his last attacking unit.
We have seen this idea again and again.

19	a6-a5

This move looks odd at first glance. But White threatens 20 Ra1-f1,
21 Bc2xg6 f7xg6, 22 Rf6xg6 mate. Therefore, Black must find a way
to bolster g6, which he does with the a-Rook! Of course, Black
couldn't have played 19 . . . Be7xf6 as after 20 Bg5xf6, mate on h8
cannot be stopped.

20 Ra1-f1	Ra8-a6
21 Bc2xg6!!	....

The breakthrough. With a winning combination, White exposes the
Black King by a piece sacrifice.

21	f7xg6
22 Rf6xf8+	Be7xf8
23 Rf1xf8+!	Kg8xf8
24 Qh4-h8+	Kf8-f7
25 Qh8-h7+	Kf7-f8

Unfortunately, Black must lose his Queen as 25 . . . Kf7-e6 is met by
26 Qh7xg6 mate and 25 . . . Kf7-e8 is answered by 26 Qh7-g8 mate.
Now we can clearly see the value of preserving the Bishop on g5!

26 Qh7xd7	Resigns

Mate follows after 27 Bg5-h6+.

The position in Figure 9-44 is somewhat similar to the previous
one, with the major difference that castling has taken place on
opposite sides. Opposite side castling gives rise to spirited attacks in

Figure 9-44   Rubinstein-Teichmann
(Vienna, 1908).

the form of Pawn storms—the players may thrust forward their wing
Pawns without fear of weakening their own Kings' defenses, which
would be the case if castling had taken place on the same side.

The key to this kind of position is simply to get to your
opponent's King first. Therefore, timing is very important. Anything
which speeds up your attack is an asset. In Figure 9-44, White
already has his kingside Pawns rolling.

13	Bg5xf6	Nd7xf6
14	g2-g4	Be7-d6
15	g4-g5	Nf6-e4
16	h4-h5	Qd8-e7
17	Rd1-g1	a7-a6

Black's Pawn storm prepared by this move is too late. White now has
a line-opening piece sacrifice which settles the issue. Such a sacrifice is typical in positions where the castled fortress has no weak
points (that is, Pawns moved). The sacrifice is even necessary in
order to prevent a blockade which would result from further Pawn
advances, for example, if 18 h5-h6 g7-g6, or if 18 g5-g6 f7xg6,
19 h5xg6 h7-h6, White finds it difficult to open lines.

18	Bf5xh7+!	Kg8xh7
19	g5-g6+	Kh7-g8
20	Nc3xe4	d5xe4

20 ... Qe7xe4 puts the Queen on a poor square, because White then has 21 g6xf7+ Kg8xf7, 22 Nf3-g5+ which wins the Queen.

21 h5-h6!!   ....

The Pawn storm has reached its climax, and the White Rooks will reap the harvest.

Figure 9-45   The crisis. Does Black have a defense?

21 ....   **f7-f6?**

Black cannot play 21 ... e4xf3, as 22 g6xf7+ Qe7xf7, 23 h6xg7! (better than 23 Rg1xg7+) with threats on h7 and h8. But the best defense would be 21 ... f7xg6, so that White would have to choose 22 Nf3-h4 with an unclear position; if 22 Rg1xg6 e4xf3! 23 Rg6xg7+ Kg8-h8! (keeping the h-file closed), Black would have more than enough material in exchange for the Queen (Rook plus Bishop plus Knight).

22 h6xg7	e4xf3
23 Rh1xh8+	Kg8xg7
24 Rh8-h7+	Kg7-g8
25 Qc2-f5!	....

The difference between the game and the variations in the last note is obvious; after winning the Queen, the attack still rages because of the presence of the g-pawn.

25	c4-c3
26 Rh7xe7	Resigns

The finish could be 26 ... Re8xe7 (26 ... Bd6xe7, 27 Qf5-e6+), 27 Qf5xf6 Bd6-b4, 28 Rg1-h1 Re7-g7, 29 Qf6-e6+, followed by mate.

In the following game, we are treated to a fine example of the use of **passed Pawns** in the middle game. White sacrifices a piece to expose the Black King and obtains some very strong passed Pawns that push on relentlessly.

Pillsbury—Wolf
(Monte Carlo, 1902)

1 d2-d4	Ng8-f6
2 c2-c4	e7-e6
3 Nb1-c3	b7-b6?

Black must contest e4 with either 3 ... Bf8-b4 or 3 ... d7-d5. Now White dominates the center.

4 e2-e4	Bc8-b7
5 Bf1-d3	d7-d5
6 c4xd5	e6xd5
7 e4-e5	Nf6-e4
8 Ng1-f3	Bf8-e7
9 0-0	0-0
10 Qd1-c2	Ne4xc3
11 Bd3xh7+!	Kg8-h8
12 b2xc3	g7-g6
13 Bh7xg6	f7xg6
14 Qc2xg6	Qd8-e8
15 Qg6-h6+	Kh8-g8
16 Nf3-g5	Be7xg5
17 Qh6xg5+	Kg8-f7

Figure 9-46   White must call in the second
wave.

The Black King sets off to find shelter on the queenside. Meanwhile, White sets his Pawns in motion.

18	f2-f4!	Kf7-e6
19	f4-f5+	Ke6-d7
20	Qg5-g7+	Kd7-c8
21	e5-e6	Rf8-g8
22	Qg7-h7	Rg8-h8
23	Qh7-g6!	Bb7-a6

Black suffers from development problems. 23 ... Qe8xg6 loses to 24 f5xg6 Rh8-g8, 25 g6-g7!

24	Qg6xe8!+	Rh8xe8
25	Rf1-e1	Nb8-c6
26	Bc1-g5	Nc6-d8
27	Bg5xd8	Kc8xd8
28	f5-f6	Re8-h8

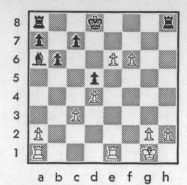

Figure 9-47   Position after 28 ... Re8-h8.
Culmination of White's strategy: the Pawns
are decisive.

29 Re1-e5	c7-c6
30 Ra1-e1	Ra8-c8
31 Re5-g5	....

Note how White obtains maximum activity for his pieces. If now
31 ... Kd8-e8, 32 Rg5-g7 is crushing.

31	Ba6-d3
32 Re1-e5	Rh8-h6
33 Rg5-g8+	Kd8-c7
34 Rg8xc8+	Kc7xc8
35 e6-e7	Bd3-g6
36 e7-e8(Q)+	Resigns

After 36 ... Bg6xe8, 37 Re5xe8+ Kc8-d7, 38 f6-f7 forces Black
to give up his Rook to stop White from promoting.

The combinational art

The synthesis of tactics and strategy reaches its pinnacle in the
chess combination. Combinations fascinate amateurs and profes-
sionals alike. Indeed, they alone attract many people to chess. How
can you learn to spot them?

A combination is a series of moves, usually containing a sacrifice, which has as its ultimate aim either winning material or

producing checkmate. It is often made up of many different tactical elements, such as those covered in Chapter 8. It arises from a position of strength—you must have certain strategic advantages, such as better development, control of the center, more space, and so on, or your opponent must have made a critical mistake, such as failing to castle or leaving pieces unprotected, in order for a combination to be present. Combinations do not magically appear: they arise in positions obtained by adhering to the principles of sound play. These principles have already been touched upon in previous chapters and will be discussed further in the next chapter.

In the following example, White has pursued a quick attack of the Black King at the expense of castling (Figure 9-48). He now should play 16 0-0-0 Ra8-c8, 17 Nd4-b3, though after Qa5-e5! Black has a good game. Instead, White sees a tactical idea, but it fails to a deep Black combination because White has ignored an important general principle: Castle to get your King out of the center.

Figure 9-48   Jaskiewicz-Savage (Baltimore, 1968).

16 Nd4-b3	Qa5-a6
17 e4-e5?	....

On general principles, this move should be bad, since it breaks open the center where White's King resides. But it was too late for 17 0-0-0, because Rc4xc3!, 18 b2xc3 (18 Qd2xc3? Nf6-d5!) Qa6xa2, gives Black a good attack.

White's tactical idea behind 17 e4-e5 appears on 17 ... d6xe5?,

18 g4-g5, and White wins the Knight on f6 or Bishop on d7. But Black's combination refutes the text.

17	**Nf6xg4!!**
18 f3xg4	**Bd7xg4**

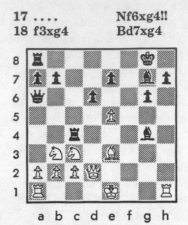

Figure 9-49   White should consolidate; instead he gets greedy.

If you recall the last section on attacking the uncastled King, Black's idea should not be a surprise—first the King must be prevented from castling. Black is now threatening to capture a third Pawn for the piece (Bg7xe5—material equality), followed by an attack with all his pieces (Ra8-f8, Be5-g3, Qa6-c6). White should now play 19 Qd2-d5+ Kg8-h8, 20 Ke1-d2!, connecting his Rooks (and developing them) with attacking chances down the h-file. Instead, he tries to hold on to his material advantage and overlooks the major point of Black's combination.

19 e5xd6   Rc4xc3!

This cashes in on the exposed nature of the White King. If now 20 b2xc3 Bg7xc3, 21 Qd2xc3 Qa6-e2 mate.

20 Be3-d4   Qa6-c6!

The final blow. Black centralizes his Queen, threatening both Qc6xh1+ and Qc6-e4+. If 21 Qd2xc3 Qc6xh1+, 22 Ke1-d2 Qh1-g2+, and so on. The exposed King is no match for the Black pieces.

21	Rh1-h2	Qc6-e4+
22	Ke1-f2	Ra8-f8+
23	Kf2-g1	Rc3-g3+
24	Rh2-g2	Rg3xg2+
25	Qd2xg2	Bg7xd4+
26	Nb3xd4	Qe4xd4+

Now White must lose his Queen as 27 Kg1-h1 is met by Bg4-f3.

27	Kg1-h2	Rf8-f2
28	d6xe7	Rf2xg2+
29	Kh2xg2	Qd4-e4+
30	Kg2-g3	Bg4-d7
31	Ra1-f1	Qe4xe7
32	Resigns	

The next example illustrates several tactical tricks interwoven in a slashing attack. The key features of the position in Figure 9-50 are the exposed King and the unprotected state of Black's Rook on f6. White needs only to find a way to activate his kingside pieces.

Figure 9-50   Mason-Winawer (Vienna, 1982).

1	Rg3xg5!	h6xg5
2	Qh5-h7+	Nc5-d7

This is forced, since 2 ... Kc7-d8, 3 Qh7-h8+ Kd8-e7, 4 Qh8-g7+ Rf6-f7, 5 f5-f6+! loses at once.

3 Bc6xd7   ....

Now the first point of White's combination appears. After 3 ... Qc8xd7, 4 Qh7xd7+ Kc7xd7, 5 Rb4xb8 leads to a won Rook and Pawn ending for White. But Black has:

3 ....   Qc8-g8!

This forces White to unveil his real point.

4 Rb4-b7+!!   Kc7xb7

Not 4 ... Rb8xb7, 5 Qh7xg8.

5 Bd7-c8+!   Resigns

A fatal double check. After 5 ... Kb7xc8 6 Qh7xg8+, Black also loses his Rook on f6.

This combination was rather forcing. At each move, Black had few choices. Such combinations, though somewhat difficult for the novice to see in advance, are really not that hard once you become very familiar with a storehouse of tactical motifs (pins, forks, double attacks, and the like). The ability to see ahead will come with experience and hard work. Do not be concerned with this now.

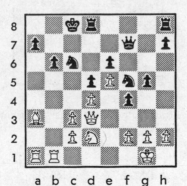

Figure 9-51   Savage-Hartman
(Correspondence, 1978).

Another kind of combination is one which a player strives for a certain position in which the opponent is so tied up that he has no defense to a long range threat. In Figure 9-51, White's pieces are more active, but Black's kingside Pawn storm needs only a few more moves to hit home. With no Pawn storm available (c3-c4 being inadequate since d4 falls), White is forced to find a queenside breakthrough with his pieces.

1 Ba3-c5!   Rd8-d7?

Of course, Black could not play b6xc5, because 2 Qd3-a6+ followed by 3 Rb1-b7+ wins. But the text is inadequate to prevent the breakthrough. Necessary was 1 . . . Qf7-c7.

2	Bc5xb6	a7xb6
3	Ra1-a8+	Nc6-b8
4	Qd3-a6+	Rd7-b7
5	Rb1xb6	. . . .

Figure 9-52   Black is fatally pinned.

Black is tied down by a variety of pins, but what is White threatening besides the e-Pawn? Simply Nd2-b3-a5-c6, followed by Ra8xb8+!— and Black does not have an adequate defense. The counterattack 5...Nf5-e3! with the idea of 6 f2xe3? f4xe3, 7 Nd2-f3 g5-g4!, or meeting 6 Nd2-b3 with Ne3-c4 is met by 6 c3-c4! threatening c4-c5-c6! If then 6 . . . Ne3xc4, 7 Nd2xc4, d5xc4, 8 Qa6xc4+ wins.

5	Rh8-e8
6 Nd2-b3	Re8-e7
7 Nb3-a5	Re7-c7
8 Na5-c6	Rc7xc6
9 Rb6xc6+	Kc8-d8
10 Qa6-a5+	Kd8-d7

10 . . . Kd8-e7 is answered with the same move.

11 Ra8xb8	Resigns

If 11 . . . Kd7xc6, 12 Qa5-c5+ wins. If 11 . . . Rb7xb8, 12 Qa5-c7+
Kd7-e8, 13 Qc7xb8+ Ke8-e7, 14 Rc6-c7 mate.

In Figure 9-53, Black is undeveloped and cannot castle without losing the Knight on e7. However, he is threatening to get his
King to safety by . . . Ke8-f7, followed by . . . Rh8-e8 and . . . Kf7-g8,
castling by hand. White must act at once if he is to keep the
advantage.

Figure 9-53   Steinitz-von Bardeleben
(Hastings, 1895).

17 d4-d5!   . . . .

A Pawn sacrifice that activates the White Knight.

17	c6xd5
18 Nf3-d4	Ke8-f7
19 Nd4-e6	Rh8-c8
20 Qe2-g4	g7-g6

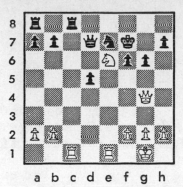

Figure 9-54   White begins an immortal combination.

White now has a grand combination that exploits Black's insecure King and unprotected Queen.

| 21 Ne6-g5+ | Kf7-e8 |
| 22 Re1xe7+!! | Ke8-f8! |

Black's move is forced but looks very good nevertheless. Now all of White's pieces are *en prise*, and he is threatened with mate in one. Black could not have played 22 ... Qd7xe7, since 23 Rc1xc8+, etc., will leave White a piece ahead. But Steinitz saw a little bit further:

| 23 Re7-f7+!! | Kf8-g8 |
| 24 Rf7-g7+ | Kg8-h8 |

Black cannot take the Rook with the King, because he loses his Queen with check. And on 24 ... Kg8-f8, 25 Ng5xh7+ wins.

25 Rh7xh7+	Kh8-g8
26 Rh7-g7+	Kg8-h8
27 Qg4-h4+	Kh8xg7
28 Qh4-h7+	Kg7-f8
29 Qh7-h8+	Kf8-e7
30 Qh8-g7+	Ke7-e8
31 Qg7-g8+	Ke8-e7
32 Qg8-f7+	Ke7-d8

On 32 ... Ke7-d6, 33 Qf7xf6+ is curtains.

33	Qf7-f8+	Qd7-e8
34	Ng5-f7+	Kd8-d7
35	Qf8-d6 mate	

The key feature of the above combination was that everything was done with check, so Black had no time to carry out any of his threats. This is a common type of situation to watch out for when one player has an exposed King.

THE ENDGAME

Though tactical play in the endgame is far less common and spectacular than in the middle game, it is important nevertheless. We shall look at two main endgame areas where it is found—promotion of passed Pawns and creation of mating attacks.

Utilization of passed Pawns

The endgame is the stage of the game where Pawns assume greater value because of the opportunity for promotion. Much of the strategy in the endgame is concerned with creating passed Pawns, and most of the tactics involve striving to promote them. Whenever you have a far-advanced passed Pawn, combinations often exist that

Figure 9-55   Fine-Keres (AVRO Tournament, 1938).

lead to promotion, so you should make every effort to look for such combinations.

In Figure 9-55, White can maintain material equality with 27 Nd4xf5, but instead sees an apparently strong tactical idea. Unfortunately, Black refutes it by realizing the power of some passed Pawns.

27 Bc1-d2?   ....

White's threat is 28 Bd2xb4, followed by 29 Nd4-c6, forking two pieces. Yet Black allows it.

27	**d6-d5!**
28 Bd2xb4	**Rb8xb4**
29 Nd4-c6	**d5xc4!**
30 Nc6xb4	**c4xb3**

The position has been drastically transformed. Black has given up the Exchange, but has obtained two valuable passed Pawns (b3 and c7) and proceeds relentlessly to promote them.

31 Nb4-d5   Nc5-d3!

32 Nd5xe7 is now impossible because of Nd3-f4+; if instead 32 Re2xe7, then b3-b2.

32 Re2-d2	**b3-b2**
33 Rd2-d1	**c7-c5?**

Easier is 33 ... Nd3-c1, 34 Nd5-c3 Be7-b4, 35 Nc3-b1 c7-c5, 36 Kg2-f1 c5-c4, winning for Black.

34 Rd1-b1	**c5-c4**
35 Kg2-f1	**Be7-c5**
36 Kf1-e2	**Bc5xf2**
37 Nd5-e3	**....**

Now it looks as if the Pawns are finally stopped, since if 37 ... Bf2xe3, then 38 Ke2xe3, followed by 39 Ke3-d4, but Black has another combination quite typical of such positions.

$$37 \ldots \ldots \qquad c4\text{-}c3!$$

White cannot play either 38 Ke2xd3 Bf2xe3, 39 Kd3xe3 c3-c2, nor 38 Ke2xd3 Bf2xe3, 39 Kd3xc3 Be3-c1 and Black wins by bringing up the King on the kingside.

$$38 \text{ Ne3-c2} \qquad \text{Nd3-e1!}$$

Anything to break the blockade of the passed Pawns.

$$39 \text{ Nc2-a3} \qquad \ldots \ldots$$

Black could have won by ... Bf2-h4 (threatening c3-c2 again), 40 Ke2-d1 Ne1xf3, and advancing the kingside Pawns. Instead Black played 39 ... Bf2-c5, but won after White missed a drawing chance later.

Figure 9-56 arose just after the exchange of Queens. Black has sacrificed a piece for two Pawns, but has a powerhouse on e2 plus the initiative.

Figure 9-56   Botvinnik-Tal (Moscow, 1960).

$$26 \ldots \ldots \qquad \text{Rc4-d4}$$
$$27 \text{ Bd2-e1} \qquad \ldots \ldots$$

On 27 Bd2-e3 Rc8xc3!, 28 Rb3xc3 Rd4-d1 ends the game at once. Such combinations with passed Pawns on the seventh rank are common.

27	....	Bg7-e5+
28	Kh2-g1	Bc5-f4

Tal missed an immediate win with 28 . . . Rc8xc3!, 29 Rb3xc3 Rd4-d1, 30 Rc3-c4 Be5-b2! (see Figure 9-57). Even though White is a Rook ahead in this analysis, he can do nothing to avoid heavy material losses. Such is the power of a passed Pawn!

Figure 9-57   After 30 . . . Be5-b2! (analysis)

Play continues:

29	Nc3xe2	Rc8xc1
30	Ne2xd4	Rc1xe1+
31	Bg2-f1	Bf5-e4

Black won with his extra Pawn.

Mating attacks

Mating attacks in the endgame are not very common, since there is so little material left on the board. Yet in certain kinds of positions, such attacks do arise. You should learn to recognize the main characteristics of those positions.

As pointed out in an earlier chapter, the King should be brought directly into the center of the board once the endgame is reached. If you fail to do this, in addition to not using that piece, you may find the King cut off on the edge and prone to an attack. The following instructive ending points out the dangers very clearly.

Figure 9-58 Ahola-Savage (Cambridge, Mass., 1979).

The position in Figure 9-58 was reached just after an exchange of Queens slowed down Black's kingside attack. The better placed Black pieces ensure an enduring initiative. Correct now would be 35 ... Nf4-g6, 36 Kh2-g3 Bf5-g4, 37 Bf1-g2 Bg4xd1!, 38 Ra1xd1 Rf8-f4 with advantage to Black. Instead Black chooses the wrong file to penetrate with his Rook and allowed the White pieces to get active play.

35	Rf8-e8
36 Nd1-c3	Re8-e3
37 Nc3-b5	Nf4-g6
38 Nb5xc7	Ng6-e5

Black threatens 39 ... Ne5-g4+, 40 Kh2-g1 Bf5-e4 with a mating net.

39 Bf1-g2	Ne5xc4?

Correct is 39 ... Ne5-g4+, 40 Kh2-g1 Re3-e2, keeping the White King confined instead of recovering the Pawn at once. The difference will be obvious in a few moves.

40 Ra1-f1!	Bf5-g4?

The active 40 ... Bf5-e4 was obviously best. Now the Black Bishop is a bystander for the rest of the game. You must keep your pieces active at all times.

41	b2-b3	Nc4-e5
42	Nc7-e8	Re3-e2?

Correct was 42 . . . Ne5-f3+ with a draw the likely result.

43	Kh2-g3!	. . . .

Activation of the King is the winning idea. The Black King cannot take part in the action and will become a target for all the White pieces.

43	. . . .	Re2xa2
44	Ne8xd6	Ra2-a3??

The final error. After 44 . . . Ra2-b2!, 45 Bg2-e4 Rb2xb3+, 46 Kg3-f4 Ne5-d7 leaves the result uncertain. After the text, the White Rook finds a quick entrance and weaves a mating net with the aid of the White King!

45	Kg3-f4	Ne5-d7
46	Rf1-e1!	Ra3xb3
47	Re1-e8+	Kg8-g7
48	Re8-e7+	Kg7-g8
49	Bg2-e4	Rb3-b4
50	Re7-e8+	Kg8-g7
51	Re8-e7+	Kg7-f8
52	Re7-e8+	Kf8-g7
53	Kf4-g5!	a5-a4

Black misses White's combination. But after the better 53 . . . Rb4-b6, 54 Nd6-c4 Rb6-a6, 55 Be4-f5! White still has good winning chances since the d-Pawn is very fast.

54	Re8-e7+	Kg7-f8
55	Re7-f7+	Kf8-g8
56	Be4-h7+	Kg8-h8
57	Kg5-h6	Rb4-b6

It looks as if White has blundered . . .

58	Rf7-f6!!	. . . .

Figure 9-59   A brilliant interference.

White brilliantly breaks the pin of his Knight. If now 58 . . . Nd7xf6, 59 Nd6-f7 mate.

58	Rb6xd6
59 Rf6xd6	a4-a3
60 Rd6-g6	Resigns

    The most common endgames are pure Rook endings, and here we find the greatest number of examples of mating attacks. This arises because the Rook is easily able to keep the King confined. In addition, the attacking force of King plus Rook and passed Pawn often leads to mating nets. One of the most famous examples is

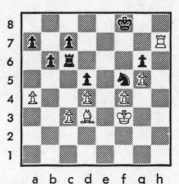

Figure 9-60   Capablanca-Tartakower
(New York, 1924).

illustrated in Figure 9-60. White's control of the seventh rank keeps the Black King confined, but White's queenside pawns are weak and seem about to fall. What can White do?

34	Bd3xf5	g6xf5
35	Kf3-g3!!	....

White's main advantage is his mobile King, so he proceeds to use it. This, coupled with White's passed g-pawn and active Rook, creates serious mating threats.

35	....	Rc6xc3+
36	Kg3-h4	Rc3-f3
37	g5-g6	Rf3xf4+
38	Kh4-g5	....

Now Black cannot take the d-pawn as 38 ... Rf4xd4, 39 Kg5-f6 Kf8-g8 (or Kf8-e8, 40 Rh7-h8+ Ke8-d7, 41 g6-g7, and Black must give up his Rook to stop the White Pawn), 40 Rh7-d7 and mates next.

38	....	Rf4-e4
39	Kg5-f6	....

White uses the f-pawn to shield the King from checks by the Black Rook. For this reason, 39 Kg5xf5 is wrong.

39	....	Kf8-g8
40	Rh7-g7+	Kg8-h8
41	Rg7xc7	Re4-e8
42	Kf6xf5	....

White now cashes in on his big positional advantage, consisting of his active king.

42	....	Re8-e4
43	Kf5-f6!	Re4-f4+
44	Kf6-e5	Rf4-g4
45	g6-g7+	Kh8-g8

The King and Pawn ending after 45 ... Rg4xg7, 46 Rc7xg7 Kh8xg7 47 Ke5xd5 is hopeless. You should work this out for yourself.

46 Rc7xa7	Rg4-g1
47 Ke5xd5	Rg1-c1
48 Kd5-d6	Rc1-c2
49 d4-d5	Rc2-c1
50 Ra7-c7	Rc1-a1
51 Kd6-c6	Ra1xa4
52 d5-d6	Resigns

The next example in Figure 9-61 is also rather typical. White has an extra Pawn, but they are weak and the King is very badly placed. Black uses the tactical threats of mate to create a winning positional advantage.

Figure 9-61   Zhidkov-Razuvaev (USSR, 1971).

| 1 .... | Kf5-f4! |

This is much stronger than 1 ... Kf5xe6, since Black's latent threat of ... g6-g5+ and ... Rd3-h3 mate ties down the White Rook to the fifth rank.

| 2 a2-a4 | Rd3-a3 |
| 3 Ra5-d5 | Ra3-a2! |

Driving the White Rook to a more passive position before capturing the a-pawn.

4 h2-h3	Ra2-a3

Now Black threatens h7-h6 followed by g6-g5+, so White's move is forced.

5 Rd5-g5	Ra3xa4
6 d4-d5	....

If 6 Rg5-g4+ Kf4-f5, 7 d4-d5 Ra4xg4+, 8 h3xg4+ Kf5-e5, Kh4-g5 Ke5xd5, 10 Kg5-h6 Kd5xe6, 11 Kh6xh7 Ke6-f6 wins for Black.

6	Ra4-a5
7 Rg5-g4+	Kf4-e5
8 Kh4-g5	....

White finally gets to activate his King, but it is too late.

8	Ra5xd5
9 Kg5-h6	Ke5-f6!
10 Kh6xh7	Rd5-h5+
11 Kh7-g8	Rh5xh3
12 Rg4-g2	Rh3-h5
13 Rg2-f2+	Rh5-f5
14 Rf2-g2	Rf5-f4
15 Rg2-g1	g6-g5
16 Rg1-g2	g5-g4
17 Kg8-h7	Kf6-g5
18 Resigns	

Black's patience in not capturing the e-pawn was exemplary. Right to the end, Black maintained the better King position. In the final position, the e-pawn will now fall easily to the Black Rook. For instance, 18 Kh7-g7 Rf4-f6, 19 Rg2-e2 g4-g3, followed by using the Black King to support the passed Pawn.

Answers to Problems

Diag. 9-7	1 Qc2-c6+, forking the Black King and Rook
Diag. 9-8	1 Rc1-c5, forking the Black Bishop and Knight
Diag. 9-9	1 e4-e5!, a Pawn fork of the Black Bishop and Knight
Diag. 9-10	1 Kc3-d4, forking the Black Bishop and Knight

chapter ten
STRATEGY

THE OPENING

In the opening stage of a game, you should have three primary
objectives in mind: controlling the center, developing *all* of your
pieces, and getting your King to safety. If you avoid violating these
three principles, you can expect to reach a reasonable middle game
position. It's that simple. But how many games, even among very
strong players, are spoiled by a tempting move that violates the
general rules? Clearly, adhering to these principles is not *that* easy,
so a more detailed discussion is in order.

The center
The **center** can be loosely defined as the four central squares
pictured in Figure 10-1. In general, when speaking of the center, the
set of squares surrounding these might also be included, for a total of
sixteen squares.

Control of the center, then, consists in using your pieces and
Pawns to exert their influence on or to occupy the central squares.
When positioned in the center, pieces have a much greater range of
activity than when placed on the wing. This can be crudely demon-
strated by comparing the possible legal moves available to, say, a
Knight, when placed on e4 vs. h3. It therefore follows that you will

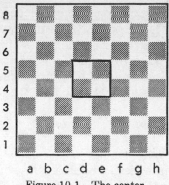

Figure 10-1   The center.

have a greater share of board control and your pieces will have greater potential, if you have better control of the center.

'The struggle for central control should begin with the first move.

You must fight for control of the center right from the opening. If the center is neglected and your opponent gains control, your pieces will have no scope and your game may never get off the ground. This is why good players strive for quick occupation of the center and develop their pieces "with an eye toward the center." Such moves as 1 e2-e4 and 1 d2-d4 are the most popular, since they immediately occupy the center and control important squares. There are other acceptable first moves (1 Ng1-f3, 1 c2-c4, 1 g2-g3), but you should avoid these for now. They are less direct and attempt to control the center from the wings, not by direct occupation with Pawns. Only after you gain experience in basic tactics and strategy will it be desirable or necessary to study those openings.

Development of forces
Developing your pieces means bringing them off the first rank and out into the open board. It is vitally important for you to learn to activate *all* of your pieces before beginning complicated middle game maneuvers. I have frequently mentioned this throughout the book, and I cannot stress it enough. Finding active squares for the major pieces as well as the minor ones is also important.

Development must be conducted in accordance with other opening principles. This means that your pieces should be developed to squares that have a bearing on the center. It is also important to avoid blocking the mobility of your center Pawns with your pieces or the development of your pieces with your Pawns. Often this requires some foresight. Look at the examples below.

1 e2-e4	e7-e5
2 Ng1-f3	Bf8-d6?

Black's move develops a piece and has bearing on the center, yet it is bad. The reason is that it blocks the mobility of the Black d-pawn. Not only will Black have difficulty developing his Bishop on c8, but this will affect the development of the whole queenside. Additionally, with only one Pawn (e5) having influence in the center, Black will be in danger of losing central control.

3 Bf1-c4	Ng8-e7

This developing move does not put enough pressure on the White center. 3 . . . Ng8-f6 is better.

4 0-0	0-0
5 c2-c3!	. . . .

Perfectly good would be developing moves such as 5 Nb1-c3, followed by d2-d3 and bringing out the Bishop on c1. But by the text move, White takes advantage of Black's immobilized d-pawn which has no influence on the center.

5	Nb8-c6
6 d2-d4	e5xd4
7 c3xd4	. . . .

It should be obvious that White now has a clear advantage. His center Pawns are mobile, and Black's further development is difficult. Another example follows.

1 d2-d4	d7-d5
2 Nb1-d2?	. . . .

This move is not very good because it blocks the further development of White's Bishop on c1 and Queen. It does threaten to play e2-e4, but Black easily prevents this with a developing move.

2	....	Ng8-f6
3	Ng1-f3	Bc8-f5
4	e2-e3	e7-e6
5	Bf1-e2	Bf8-d6
6	0-0	c7-c5
7	c2-c3	0-0

White's opening play has been very passive compared to Black's. It is enough to compare the scope of the respective Queen's Bishops (Black's on f5, White's on c1) to see this. Note how Black first developed his Bishop to f5, *then* played e7-e6 and followed by developing the Bishop on f8. White, on the other hand, played e2-e3 before developing the Bishop on c1 and thus finds it blocked in by his own Pawns on e3, d4, and c3.

Castling

Castling serves two purposes: (1) to get the King out of the center into relative safety and (2) to bring the Rooks into the center. Thus you can see that castling is a developing move for the Rooks.

The rationale behind castling is simple—most of the action takes place in the center. Therefore, it is logical to remove the King from this sensitive area early in the game. Usually some center Pawns are exchanged early. This produces open and half-open files where the Rooks can best be utilized. Bringing the Rooks to the center by castling, then, places the Rooks where they are likely to become active.

Earlier in the book, I showed how your King can be attacked if you fail to castle early. Just as deadly are tactical tricks that arise because of the open center files. A common example follows:

1	e2-e4	e7-e5
2	Ng1-f3	Nb8-c6
3	Bf1-b5	Ng8-f6
4	0-0	Nf6xe4
5	d2-d4	e5xd4?

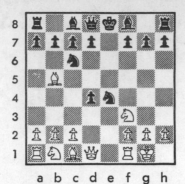

Figure 10-2   White exploits the open
e-file.

Black fails to realize he is neglecting development and is tempted by
Pawn captures. His last opens the e-file and allows White to win
material.

6 Rf1-e1	d7-d5
7 Nf3xd4	....

White has two threats: 8 Nd4xc6 b7xc6 9 Bb5xc6+ winning the
Exchange, and the threat on the e-file. Black cannot stop both.

7	Bc8-d7
8 Bb5xc6	b7xc6
9 f2-f3	....

White wins a piece.

One further example concerning castling and opening strategy
should be mentioned. On occasion, there will occur an opening
position where early castling is not necessary. This occurs when the
center is blocked, and there is little chance that a file will open there.
In such positions, most of the play will take place on the flank, and
the King will often be safer in the center. Look at the following
opening variation:

1 e2-e4	e7-e6
2 d2-d4	d7-d5

3 e4-e5	c7-c5
4 c2-c3	Nb8-c6
5 Ng1-f3	Qd8-b6

It is generally wrong to develop the Queen early in the game, because it can be harrassed easily. In the present variation, however, the center is closed and the minor pieces have less mobility than in most games. Black's 5 ... Qd8-b6 is a good move, because it attacks White's center (d4) and the Queen cannot be easily attacked.

| 6 Bf1-e2 | c5xd4 |
| 7 c3xd4 | Ng8-h6 |

This move may look odd, but the Knight, denied "normal" access to the f6 square, must find another method of developing. It is heading for f5 in order to attack the center Pawn at d4.

8 b2-b3	Nh6-f5
9 Bc1-b2	Bf8-b4+
10 Ke1-f1	....

Figure 10-3 Loss of castling: when it doesn't matter.

White must move his King, since any move which blocks the check loses the d-pawn. So White has lost the right to castle. But is this so bad in the present position? There is little chance that the center will open quickly, so the King is relatively safe here. Furthermore, White may play an eventual g2-g3 followed by Kf1-g2, castling by hand if necessary. The only other drawback to White's loss of castling is the difficult time he will have developing the Rook on h1. But if the game remains closed for some time, the Rooks will have no files to operate on anyhow.

In sum, closed positions (locked Pawns, especially in the center) allow you to bend general principles quite a bit. These positions are not that common in the games of a novice, but you should at least learn to recognize them.

THE MIDDLE GAME

A comprehensive discussion of middle game strategy is beyond the scope of this book and the requirements of the beginning player. However, it is important for the novice to develop an understanding of a framework for future middle game study. To this end, I will present a discussion of what I believe is the fundamental component upon which all middle game theories are based: Pawn structure. I have also included a discussion of space as a starting point for more advanced work.

Pawn Structure

Pawn structure is to a chess game what the skeleton is to the human body. The Pawn structure gives the position shape and a solid framework on which to build an elaborate edifice. Middle game operations,

Figure 10-4 From the Sicilian Defense.　Figure 10-5 From the French Defense.

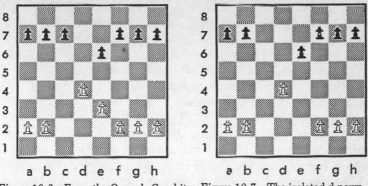

Figure 10-6   From the Queen's Gambit.   Figure 10-7   The isolated d-pawn.

which comprise the meat of most games, are highly dependent upon and developed directly in response to the nature of the Pawn structure.

When discussing the important aspects of the Pawn structure, it is often useful to visualize the position of the Pawns by themselves with the pieces removed, as seen in Figure 10-4 to 10-7. Let's examine these four typical formations to illustrate how the middle game plans are determined by the Pawn structure. Our major concern will be to learn to recognize the following four aspects of each position we examine:

1. Open files and half-open files
2. Pawn majorities
3. Advanced Pawns
4. Weak squares

Open files and half-open files

A completely **open file** is one on which no player has a Pawn in place. A **half-open file** is one on which only one player has a Pawn. A file is considered half-open for the player without the Pawn. Thus, there are no open files in Figures 10-4 to 10-6 and an open c-file in Figure 10-7. In Figure 10-4, White has a half-open d-file and Black a half-open c-file. In Figure 10-6, White has a half-open c-file and Black a half-open d-file. In Figure 10-7, White has a half-open e-file and Black a half-open d-file. There are no half-open files in Figure 10-5.

Since the Rooks (and often the Queen) can exert their maximum effect on open and half-open files, they should be stationed on such files. If a position has no open or half-open files, the Rooks should be positioned on a file which is likely to open. Files open up by Pawn exchanges or Pawn captures. Therefore, you must determine where Pawn exchanges are likely to take place, or more commonly, make the Pawn exchanges first and then position your Rooks.

When you have understood the foregoing, then you will not be surprised to find the typical placement of the White and Black Rooks in Figure 10-8. Each side has placed a Rook on its half-open file. The remaining Rooks are placed on files that are likely to open up by Pawn exchanges: Black's d-file by d6-d5 and White's f-file by f4-f5.

Figure 10-8   Typical Rook placement in the Sicilian.

In Figure 10-5, it seems difficult to determine the correct placement of the Rooks. But it is really very easy: The Pawn structure in the center is locked up in such a way that Pawn exchanges will most likely occur only on the f-file or b-file. White may play b2-b3 or f2-f4-f5. The first will result in a half-open b-file for White, and the second in a half-open f-file. Therefore, the placement of the White Rooks on the b- and f-files is indicated. Black's Pawn breaks are found in b7-b5-b4 or f7-f6, so Rook placement should likewise be clear.

The likely Pawn breaks in Figure 10-5 also suggest another

Rook placement. For example, if Black plays f7-f6 and White answers e5xf6, White's e-file will be half-open. Therefore, a White Rook placed on e1 seems reasonable. Similarly, a Black Rook on c8 may deter a future b2-b3 by White.

A look at the Pawn structure indicates the location of the open and half-open files and thus suggests the correct placement for the Rooks. In addition, determining the location of future Pawn exchanges will tell you where new files may be opened.

Pawn majorities

If one player has more Pawns than his or her opponent on one side of the board, then that player is said to have a Pawn majority. In Figure 10-9, White has a four to three Pawn majority on the kingside and Black a three to two Pawn majority on the queenside. (If you have difficulty visualizing this, remove everything from the board except the Pawns.) Recognizing the existence of Pawn majorities will help you to formulate a plan. Generally speaking, you should attack or play actively on the side of the board where you have a Pawn majority. Thus, in Figure 10-9, White should pursue a plan of advancing the kingside Pawns by preparing f2-f4 and e4-e5.

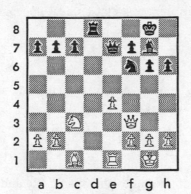

Figure 10-9   Mobilizing Pawn majorities.

Contrast the Pawn structure in Figure 10-9 with that in Figure 10-6. There are no clear Pawn majorities in Figure 10-6, but if White's d-pawn were exchanged for Black's e-pawn, Pawn majorities similar to Figure 10-9 would result. Let's look at some possible

continuations from Figure 10-9 to illustrate how Pawn majorities can
be mobilized.

	1 Qf3-e2	Qe7-c5?
	2 e4-e5!	Nf6-d5
	3 e5-e6!	f7xe6

If 3 ... Nd5xc3, 4 e6xf7+ Kg8xf7, 5 Qe2-e6+ Kf7-f8, 6 b2xc3, and
the Black King is very exposed.

	4 Qe2xe6+	Kg8-h7
	5 Nc3-e4	....

It is clear that White has good attacking chances against Black's
weakened kingside. Another line might go as follows:

	1 Qf3-e2	c7-c6
	2 f2-f4	b7-b5
	3 e4-e5	Nf6-d5
	4 Nc3-e4	....

And White is better. Perhaps Black's best approach in Figure 10-9
is:

	1 Qf3-e2	Nf6-d7

This is played to hinder e4-e5, because if now 2f2-f4, then
2 ... Nd7-c5, with the idea of ... Nc5-d3.

	2 Nc3-d5	Qe7-d6
	3 Re1-d1	....

With 3 Re1-d1, White occupies the open d-file and will continue the
strategic plan of f2-f4 to mobilize the Pawn majority.

Advanced Pawns

An **advanced Pawn** refers to any Pawn which is on its own
fifth rank or beyond. Such Pawns greatly affect the middle game
plans for both sides, since they confer a space advantage on the

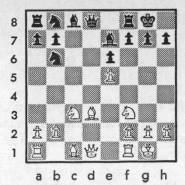

Figure 10-10 White has a space advantage.

possessor of the advanced Pawn. In Figure 10-5, the Pawn on e5 gives White a space advantage on the kingside and the advanced c-pawn gives Black a space advantage on the queenside. Generally, you should direct your attack to the side of the board where your space advantage lies. Figure 10-10 shows an excellent example. White's Pawn on e5 cuts the Black position in two. The Pawn's control of the f6 square hinders Black's pieces from defending the castled position. Most specifically, without a protective Knight on f6, the h7 square is quite vulnerable to an attack by the White pieces.

11	Qd1-e2	Nb8-c6
12	Rf1-d1	Nb6-d5
13	Bd3-e4	Nd5xc3
14	Be4xh7+!	....

White takes the opportunity to expose the Black King because now, if 14 ... Kg8xh7, 15 Qe2-c2+, followed by Rd1xd8, Black loses his Queen.

14	....	Kg8-h8
15	b2xc3	Qd8-a5
16	Bh7-c2	Qa5xc3
17	Qe2-e4	g7-g6
18	Nf3-g5	....

Notice the focus on the vulnerable h7 square. If now 18 ... Qc3xa1,

19 Qe4-h4+ Kh8-g7, 20 Qh4-h7 mate. Also 18 ... Be7xg5 is bad, because 19 Bc1xg5, followed by Bg5-f6, will eventually mate on h8.

18	Qc3-b4
19 Ng5xf7+	....

White concludes with a destructive sacrifice, shattering the Pawn cover of the Black King. Special note should be made of the fact that Black's queenside pieces cannot help out, as a result of the cramp exerted by the advanced Pawn on e5.

19	Rf8xf7
20 Qe4xg6	Rf7-g7
21 Qg6-h5+	Kh8-g8
22 Bc1-h6	Be7-f8
23 Bh6xg7	Bf8xg7
24 Rd1-d3!	Bg7xe5
25 Rd3-f3	....

Once again, a mate threat on h7.

27	Qb4-e7
28 Qh5-g6+	Qd7-g7
29 Qg6-e8+	Resigns

In Figure 10-11, White has a small but clear advantage due to his

Figure 10-11   Tarrasch-Schiffers (Vienna, 1898).

advanced Pawn on e5. This gives him more space on the kingside
and indicates that he should play for a kingside attack. Black must
find counterplay on the other wing.

| 15 .... | f7-f5 |

Black closes the aggressive diagonal b1-h7 where the White Bishop
will be posted. It would now be wrong for White to play 16 e5xf6 *en
passant*, since his advantage derived from the e5 Pawn would be
liquidated.

16 Bf1-d3	Rc8-c7
17 0-0	Kg8-h8
18 Kg1-h1	Bd7-e8
19 h2-h3	....

White correctly continues his kingside attack, preparing g2-g4. If
now 19 ... Be8-h5, 20 Nf3-h2, followed by 21 g2-g4. Black's next
attempts to counter on the queenside with Na7-b5 or Be8-b5, but
White easily prevents this.

19	Nc6-a7
20 a2-a4	Na7-c6
21 g2-g4	g7-g6
22 a4-a5	Nb6-c8
23 Rf1-g1	Nc6-a7
24 Rg1-g3	....

Note how White prepares to control the g-file before opening it.
Black's best is now 24 ... Be8-b5, 25 g4xf5 g6xf5, 26 Ra1-g1, but
instead he prevents the opening of the g-file at the price of allowing
White's Pawns to mobilize.

24	f5xg4?
25 h3xg4	Be8-b5
26 f4-f5!	....

If now 26 ... e6xf5, 27 g4xf5 g6xf5 28 Ra1-g1, and White has good
attacking chances for the Pawn.

| 26 .... | Bb5xd3 |
| 27 f5-f6! | .... |

Figure 10-12   The powerhouse on f6 is
fatal to Black.

White establishes an advanced Pawn on the sixth rank, making
Black's King's defense impossible. This is tactically sound, because
if 27 ... Rf8xf6, 28 e5xf6 Qe7-d6, 29 Nf3-e5! Bd3xc2 (with a material advantage), there follows 30 Qd2-h6 (with the threat of
f6-f7-f8!) Kh8-g8, 31 Ra1-f1 Qd6-f8, 32 f6-f7+ Rc7xf7, 33 Ne5xf7
wins.

27	Qe7-e8
28 Qd2xd3	Na7-b5
29 Nf3-g5!	....

White offers a Queen sacrifice that must be accepted.

29	Rc7-c3
30 Qd3xc3	Nb5xc3
31 Rg3xc3	....

White now has two threats: Rc3-c7 and Rc3-h3, both of which cannot
be met. White's advanced Pawns and strong Knight make Black
helpless.

| 31 .... | h7-h6 |
| 32 Rc3-h3 | Qe8-c6 |

On 32 ... h6-h5, 33 Ra1-g1 wins.

33	Rh3xh6+	Kh8-g8
34	Rh6xg6+	Kg8-h8
35	Nc2-e1	....

There is no defense to the threat of bringing the a-Rook to the h-file.

36	....	Ng8-e7
36	Rg6-h6+	Kh8-g8
37	Ne1-g2	Qc6-c3
38	Ra1-e1	Ne7-c6
39	Rh6-g6+	Kg8-h8
40	Re1-e3	Qc3xe3
41	Ng2xe3	Resigns

Weak squares

A weak square or **hole** is a square in the opponent's position which cannot be guarded by a Pawn. Such squares are ripe for occupation by your pieces and constitute a defect in the opponent's Pawn structure. For instance, in Figure 10-5 White has a hole at b3, and in Figure 10-7 White has a hole on d5. A fine example of the exploitation of weak squares is found in Figure 10-13. A gaping hole in the Black position exists on c5 and is thus ripe for occupation by White's pieces. Note that White has a half-open c-file.

Figure 10-13   Huebner-Gligoric (Skopje, 1972).

15	Rf1-e1	Rf8-e8
16	Bb2-c3	Qa5-b5
17	Qd1-d2	Qb5-b8

Black is trying to free his position by ... e7-e5 since the desirable ... c6-c5 is impossible.

18	Bc3-b2	e7-e5
19	d4xe5	Nd7xe5
20	Bb2-d4!	....

All of White's pieces take aim at the c5 square.

20	....	Bg7-f8
21	Bd4-c5	Ne5-d7
22	Bc5xf8	Nd7xf8
23	Na4-c5	....

Figure 10-14   White occupies the hole at c5.

Finally, White occupies c5. So what? Look carefully at the sphere of influence that the White Knight exerts over the whole board. Pay particular attention to the fact that this Knight cannot be driven away by Pawns—such is the nature of the hole.

23	....	Qb8-e5
24	e2-e4!	d5xe4

25 Bg2xe4	Bf5xe4
26 Re1xe4	Qe5-d5
27 Qd2-e3	Re8xe4
28 Nc5xe4	Qd5-e5
29 Rc1-c5!	....

The triumph of c5. Utilization of the hole as a jumping-off point for one's whole army is quite typical.

29	Qe5-g7
30 Rc5-a5	....

White won the a-pawn and the game.

    A similar kind of weak square appears when a hole is created on a completely open file. Look at Figure 10-15. White, bothered by the pin on his Knight on e2, chooses to break it but incurs a hole at e3. Better would have been 8 Bc1-e3 followed by 9 Qd1-c1.

Figure 10-15 Yates-Nimzovich (Semmering, 1926).

8 f2-f3?	Bg4-h5
9 Ne2-f4	Bh5-g6
10 Nc3-e2	Bb4-d6
11 Qd1-e1	....

Correct according to Nimzovich was 11 Bd3xg6 h7xg6 12 Nf4-d3 preventing ... c7-c5.

11	c7-c5!
12 d4xc5	Bd6xc5+
13 Kg1-h1	Nb8-c6
14 Bc1-d2	Rf8-e8

Eyeing e3.

15 Nf4xg6	h7xg6
16 f3-f4	Ne7-f5
17 c2-c3	d5-d4!
18 c3-c4	Qd8-b6
19 Rf1-f3	Bc5-b4!

Clearing a vital defender of e3.

20 a2-a3	Bb4xd2
21 Qe1xd2	a7-a5
22 Ne2-g1	Re8-e3

And Black won. See Figure 10-16, and compare the last two diagrams carefully to see how Black has exploited e3.

Figure 10-16   Black dominates the hole at e3.

I would like to close this section of the chapter with another example from Nimzovich's games. It was he who introduced the blockading strategy that is connected with the exploitation of holes. In Figure 10-17, White has no compensation for the hole at c4. He

Figure 10-17   Mannheimer-Nimzovich
(Frankfort, 1930).

establishes his own Knight on e5, but must allow another weakness
at e4.

20	Nc6-a5
21 f2-f4	....

This secures e5, but leaves Black in possession of e4. The move
21 f2-f3 would control e4, but leave White with the problem of what
to do with his Knight on h2.

21	Qg7-d7
22 Nh2-f3	Qd7-c6
23 Nf3-e5	Qc6-e6

Not 23 ... Qc6xc3, 24 Qd3xc3 Ne4xc3, 25 Bc1-d2 Nc3-e2+ 26
Kg1-f2, and Black loses a piece.

24 Ra1-b1	b7-b6
25 Kg1-h2	Na5-c4
26 Bc1-e3	g6-g5

The Black Knights' occupation of two holes outweighs the value of
the White Knight at e5. Nimzovich now proceeds to open up the
game for his Rooks and finds further weak squares on the kingside.
Notice the hole at g3 and the impotent White Bishop.

Figure 10-18   The Black Knights control the board.

27 g2-g3	Rf8-f6
28 Rb1-e1	Ra8-g8
29 Be3-c1	b6-b5
30 Ne5-f3?	....

This allows Black to create a hole at g4 and finish the game as he pleases.

30	g5-g4
31 h3xg4	Rg8xg4
32 Nf3-g1	Rf6-g6
33 Rf1-f3	Qe6-g8
34 Ng1-e2	....

Figure 10-19   White can hardly move.

The occupation of the hole at c4, e4 and g4 makes a pretty picture. The game concludes: 34 . . . h6-h5, 35 Kh2-g2 h5-h4, 36 Re1-h1 Rg6-h6, 37 Rh1-h3 Qg8-g6, 38 Bc1-e3 Qg6-a6, 39 Be3-f2 Qa6xa2, 40 Bf2-e1 a7-a5, 41 Kg2-f1 Qa2-b1, 42 Ne2-g1 a5-a4, 43 Kf1-e2 a4-a3, 44 Rf3-f1 a3-a2, White resigns.

The Advantage of Space

An advantage in space exists if one player has one or more advanced Pawns. Generally speaking, this type of advantage must be exploited in the middle game or transformed into some other advantage.

The usual way to exploit a space advantage is to concentrate one's forces and attack on the side of the board where the space advantage lies. At the same time, the player with the advantage should avoid exchanging too many pieces and prevent freeing Pawn exchanges.

The player with a space disadvantage has a cramped position. This is usually caused by the existence of the opponent's advanced Pawn. Therefore, the cramped side should strive to undermine the supports of the advanced Pawn or to create a **lever** with the Pawn itself in order to exchange it. If this can be done without creating other weaknesses, the attacker will lose his advantage in space. The cramped side should also try to trade off the opponent's attacking pieces—this will slow the attack and ease the cramp. Let's look at some examples.

In Figure 10-20, White has a space advantage on the kingside

Figure 10-20 Alekhine-Capablanca (AVRO Tournament, 1938).

because of the advanced Pawn on e5. As a consequence, Black is cramped in that region and must look for counterplay on the other wing or play ... f7-f6 to exchange off White's advanced Pawn. Since he can bring no more pressure to bear on the e-pawn's support (the Pawn at d4), ... f7-f6 is a logical try.

11 a2-a3	**Nd7-f8?**

If he does not want to play 11 ... f7-f6, then he must at least prevent White from also gaining space on the queenside via 12 b2-b4. Therefore, 11 ... a7-a5 was indicated. Under no circumstances should you ever allow your opponent to get a space advantage on both sides of the board.

12 b2-b4	**Bc8-d7**
13 Bc1-e3	**Nc6-d8**
14 Ne2-c3	**a7-a5**

Black strives to get some space on the queenside.

15 Nc3-a4	**Qb6-a7**

Better is 15 ... Bd7xa4, 16 Qd1xa4+ Nd8-c6, trading off a pair of pieces and thus easing the defense of his cramped position.

16 b4-b5!	**....**

White establishes an advanced Pawn on the queenside as well, giving him a space advantage on both sides of the board.

16	**b7-b6**
17 g2-g3	**f7-f5**
18 Kf1-g2	**Nd8-f7**
19 Qd1-d2	**h7-h6**

Black has been trying to gain some space on the kingside by playing ... g7-g5, but White stops this and then exploits the hole at g6.

20	h2-h4!	Nf8-h7
21	h4-h5	Nf7-g5
22	Nf3-h4	....

Avoiding unnecessary exchanges which would ease Black's cramp.

22	....	Ng5-e4
23	Qd2-b2	Ke8-f7

Black wants to activate his h-Rook by bringing it to c8 and thus avoids 23 ... 0-0, 24 Nh4-g6 Rf8-f7, which ties the Rook down to defense. But the plan is faulty, since White now has a breakthrough.

24	f2-f3	Ne4-g5
25	g3-g4	f5xg4
26	Bd3-g6+	Kf7-g8
27	f3-f4	Ng5-f3
28	Bg6xh7+	Rh8xh7
29	Nh4-g6!	Be7-d8
30	Ra1-c1!	....

This prevents any counterplay via Black's a-Rook getting to the open c-file.

30	....	Bd7-e8
31	Kg2-g3!	....

Black's Knight on f3 is stranded and helpless.

31	....	Qa7-f7
32	Kg3xg4	Nf3-h4
33	Ng6xh4	Qf7xh5+
34	Kg4-g3	Qh5-f7
35	Nh4-f3	Resigns

Black resigns because he is a piece down and has no compensation.

The next example (Figure 10-21) illustrates how an advantage in space can be turned into an attack on the King. White is better developed, well centralized, and has an advanced Pawn on e5 giving him a space advantage on the kingside.

Figure 10-21   Sznapik-Schmidt (Poland, 1977).

17 Nf3-d4	c7-c6
18 Be2-g4	Qc8-c7
19 Ra1-c1!	....

Note how White's last three moves have mobilized all his forces.

19	Bg6-e4
20 e5-e6!!	Be4xd5
21 Qb3xd5	....

White uses his advanced Pawn to open up the Black King. If Black now trades Queens with c6xd5, there follows 22 Rc1xc7 Be7-d6, 23 e6xf7+ Kg8-h8, 24 Rc7xb7 Nb8-a6, 25 Nd4-e6, and White recovers the Exchange, coming out two Pawns ahead with a won position.

So Black decides to keep the position closed as long as possible, hoping to be able to catch up in development and exploit his material advantage. White, however, has full compensation in his advanced passed Pawn and piece mobility. He turns this into a raging attack on the King.

21	f7-f6
22 Qd5-c4	g7-g6

This was played to keep the White Knight out of f5, but further weakens the kingside.

23 Be3-h6   Rf8-d8?

Black had to return the Exchange and catch up in development with
23 ... Nb8-a6.

24 Nd4-f5!!   ....

Black cannot capture the Knight, since after 24 ... g6xf5, 25 Bg4xf5
(threat is 26 Qc4-g4+) Kg8-h8, 26 Qc4-h4 (veiled threat of h7) Rd8-
g8, 27 Bf5xh7! wins.

Meanwhile, White threatens 25 Bh6-f4. Black must make a
square for his Queen.

24 ....   b7-b6
25 Qc4-f4!   Qc7-b7
26 Bg4-h5!   ....

Figure 10-22   White's pieces loom over the
Black King.

White has a massive concentration of forces on the kingside. Such
positions almost always contain a breakthrough if you look hard
enough for it. White wants to get into g7 and the g6 Pawn is the only
barrier. But Black has no way to prevent a sacrifice there. Of course,
he cannot now play g6xh5 or g6xf5 since Qf4-g3+ leads to mate.

26 ....   Rd8-d5
27 Qf4-g4   Rd5xf5
28 Bh5xg6   Rf5-g5

29	Bg6-f7+	Kg8-h8
30	Bh6xg5	Resigns

If 30 ... f6xg5, 31 Qg4-d4+ leads to mate. If 30 ... Nb8-a6, 31 Bg5-h6 Be7-f8, Qg4-g8 mate. You should make careful note of the cramping effect of the White advanced Pawn at e6 in this game and its subsequent role in the attack.

Remember that the Pawn structure, not necessarily the position of the opponent's King, determines where you should attack. In Figure 10-23, White has a space advantage on the queenside because of the advanced Pawn on d5. His plan is simple: Increase the queenside pressure by advancing his Pawns there. The goal is to mobilize the entire wing via the eventual advance c4-c5.

Figure 10-23   Botvinnik-Reshevsky (AVRO Tournament, 1938).

13	a2-a3	Nd7-c5
14	b3-b4	Nc5-d7

Black's last two moves have lost time.

15	Qd1-b3	Nf5-d4
16	Ne2xd4	Bg7xd4
17	Ra1-d1	Bd4-g7
18	Rf1-e1	....

Notice how White mobilizes all of his forces before undertaking any complex action. Black now decides to try and complete his development, even though it means he must relinquish control of c5.

18	a5xb4
19 a3xb4	Nd7-f6
20 h2-h3	h7-h5
21 c4-c5!	Bc8-f5
22 Nc3-b5	....

The threat is 23 Nb5-d4 Bf5-d7, 24 c5-c6! b7xc6, 25 d5xc6 Bd7-c8, 26 b4-b5 with a mobile queenside Pawn majority that will soon produce a strong passed Pawn.

22	Bf5-d7
23 c5-c6!	b7xc6
24 d5xc6	Bd7-c8

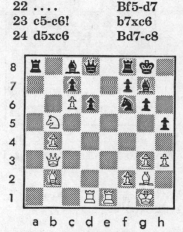

Figure 10-24 Position after 24 d5xc6
Bd7-c8. White mobilizes the advanced Pawn.

25 Nb5xd6!	....

A typical breakthrough combination, common in positions where a space advantage has been expanded to great proportions, that is, where a far advanced Pawn is established. If now 25 ... c7xd6, 26 c6-c7 wins the Rook in the corner.

25	Bc8-e6!
26 Re1xe6!	f7xe6

27 Nd6-f5!	Qd8-e8
28 Nf5xg7	Kg8xg7
29 Rd1-d7+	Rf8-f7
30 Bb2-e5	....

And White wins the c-pawn, producing two connected passed Pawns and a winning position.

Our final example in Figure 10-25 shows White with a space advantage on the queenside and Black with a very cramped game. White therefore blocks the kingside and proceeds with the now familiar systematic advance.

Figure 10-25   Maroczy-Suchting (Barmen, 1905).

| 21 g4-g5 | Nf6-d7 |
| 22 Ne5-d3! | .... |

White is careful to prevent Black from making exchanges. Note how congested Black's pieces are.

| 22 .... | Be8-f7 |
| 23 Ke1-d2 | .... |

Of course, the King is perfectly safe in the center of the board in this position, since the center cannot be opened.

23	Be7-d8
24 Rh1-a1	Bd8-c7
25 Ra1-a7	Rf8-e8

Black tries to get counterplay by threatening e6-e5.

26	Bf4xc7	Qc8xc7
27	f2-f4!	Re8-b8
28	b4-b5!	....

Figure 10-26   White puts on the squeeze.

Finally the strategic advance is played. If now 28 ... c6xb5, 29 Nd3-b4, threatening c5-c6, and Nb4-a6 is decisive.

28	....	Qc7-c8
29	b5-b6	....

The b-pawn is doomed. Black is so cramped that he cannot arrange an adequate defense.

29	....	Bf7-e8
30	Nd3-c1	Nd7-f8
31	Nc1-b3	e6-e5

This sacrifice is forced in order to swing the Knight over to defend the b-pawn as White threatens Nb3-a5xb7 (Rb8xb7 Be2-a6).

32	d4xe5	Nf8-e6
33	Be2-d3	g7-g6
34	h4-h5	Be8-f7
35	Nb3-a5	Ne6-d8

Figure 10-27   Position after 35 Nb3-a5
Ne6-d8. White switches to the kingside.

36 e5-e6!   ....

The final breakthrough. White switches to a kingside attack that
ultimately forces the win of the b-pawn.

36	Qc8xe6
37 h5-h6	d5-d4
38 Qc3xd4	Qe6-a2+
39 Kd2-e1	Nd8-e6
40 Qd4-e5	Rb8-e8
41 Na5xb7 and White won.	

THE ENDGAME

Endgame strategy is characterized by the need to create and promote passed Pawns. It is important to study and fully understand all
techniques that help you achieve this goal. This section will introduce you to three of the most important endgame principles that,
once assimilated, will greatly improve your game.

Advanced Pawns

The only concern in this part is how advanced Pawns play a
special role in the endgame. You should recall from previous discussions that advanced Pawns confer a space advantage to the

player who possesses them. In the endgame, the space advantage
and advanced Pawns can often be transformed into far advanced
passed Pawns. In Figure 10-28, Black has more active pieces, better

Figure 10-28 Merenyi-Capablanca
(Budapest, 1928).

Pawns, and a centralized position. He first immobilizes White's
Pawn majority and then proceeds to turn his kingside space advantage into a passed Pawn.

24	....	a6-a5!
25	Nd2-b1	Re7-d7
26	Nb1-d2	e5-e4!

This establishes an advanced Pawn on the kingside, guaranteeing
Black a space advantage there.

27	Nd2-b3	Nc5-d3

Of course, Black refuses to exchange pieces since he has a strategic
advantage and not a material one.

28	Nb3-d4+	Kc6-c5
29	b2-b3	f7-f5
30	Ra3-a1	Rd7xd4!

Figure 10-29   Position after 30 Ra3-a1.
Black sacrifices to activate his Pawns.

An Exchange sacrifice proves to be the simplest way to exploit the
advanced Pawn majority on the kingside. The rapid mobilization of
Black's passed Pawns is the key to the concept.

31	e3xd4+	Kc5xd4
32	g2-g3	g6-g5!
33	b3-b4	....

White will do anything to open up some files for Rook activity. For
instance, if now 33 ... a5xb4, 34 a4-a5 or 33 ... Nd3xb4, 34 Ra1-d1+.
But Black can safely ignore White's counterplay, because his kingside Pawns are too fast. This is a direct benefit from his advanced
Pawn and space advantage.

33	....	f5-f4!
34	c4-c5	f4-f3+
35	Ke2-f1	e4-e3
36	Ra1-e1	....

Desperation, since 36 c5xb6 e3-e2+, 37 Kf1-g1 f3-f2+ forces a
Queen.

36	....	b6xc5
37	Re1xe3	Kd4xe3
38	b4xa5	c5-c4
39	White resigns	

The c-pawn promotes with checkmate!

In Figure 10-30, Black has advanced Pawns on both sides of the board and, as a consequence, White is quite cramped. Black's long range plan is to force an entrance into White's position when his advanced Pawns can be turned into passed Pawns.

Figure 10-30   Henneberger-Nimzovich (Winterthur, 1931).

26	h6-h5
27 Kg1-g2	Bc7-d6
28 Rf1-c1	h5-h4
29 Rd2-d1	....

Of course, not 29 g3xh4 Nd5xf4+, when Black can mobilize his advanced kingside Pawns.

29	Rg8-h8
30 Rd1-d2	Kf7-e7
31 Rd2-c2	Ke7-d7
32 Rc1-e1	Rh8-h7
33 Re1-a1	h4xg3?

It would have been better to play 33 ... h4-h3 +!, creating a very far advanced Pawn. Then if Black were later to win the Pawn at h2, his own h-pawn would be practically promoted. Permanently locking up the kingside with 33 ... h4-h3+ is acceptable here, because Black will be able to break through on the queenside with ... b5-b4.

Figure 10-31   The critical position.

A short time later the position in Figure 10-31 was reached. Black achieved his breakthrough with b5-b4 and now threatens to create an entrance for his King with 43 ... a4-a3, 44 b2xa3 Bb4xe1, 45 Kf1xe1 Kb5-a4, etc. If 43 Be1xb4 Kb5xb4, 44 Kf1-e1 c4-c3, 45 b2xc3 Nd5xc3, etc.

43 Ne2-c3+	Bb4xc3
44 b2xc3	....

White has temporarily prevented Black's King from penetrating. Meanwhile, Black has accumulated another strategic advantage— good Knight vs. bad Bishop.

44	Kb5-c6
45 Kf1-e2	Nd5-f6
46 Ke2-e3	Nf6-e4
47 Ke3-e2	Kc6-d5
48 Ke2-e3	Kd5-d6
49 Ke3-e2	Kd6-c6
50 Ke2-e3	Kc6-d5

Black's last King maneuvers were not aimless. He has set himself up for the final winning maneuver.

51 Ke3-e2	Ne4-d6
52 Ke2-e3	Nd6-b5
53 Be1-d2	....

White tries to keep Black's King out of e4 as long as possible.

53	Nb5-a3
54 Bd2-c1	Na3-b1!
55 Bc1-b2	a4-a3!
56 Bb2-a1	Kd5-d6
57 Ke3-e2	Kd6-c6!
58 Ke2-d1	Kc6-d5
59 Kd1-c2	Kd5-e4
60 Kc2xb1	Ke4-f3
61 Ba1-b2	a3xb2

Figure 10-32   Culmination of Black's strategy.

And here, finally, we see the value of advanced Pawns—Black's Pawns will be closer to promoting. Just barely!

62 a2-a4	Kf3xg3
63 a4-a5	Kg3-h2!!
64 a5-a6	g4-g3
65 a6-a7	g3-g2
66 a7-a8(Q)	g2-g1(Q)+
67 Kb1xb2	Qg1-g2+
68 Qa8xg2+	Kh2xg2
69 Kb2-a3	Kg2-f3
70 Ka3-b4	Kf3xf4
71 Kb4xc4	Kf4-e3
72 d4-d5	e6xd5+
73 Kc4xd5	f5-f4

And Black won.

Sometimes advanced Pawns, left over from a middle game attack on the King, serve to cramp the opponent. This factor, added to other assets, is often decisive in the endgame. A typical example is seen in Figure 10-33. The cramping effect of the Pawn at a6 sets up various mating threats as it confines the Black King. In contrast, note how the White King is centralized and can play an active role.

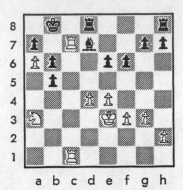

Figure 10-33   Botvinnik-Vidmar (Groningen, 1946).

Black cannot now play 33 ... b5-b4, because White has 34 Rc7-b7+ Kb8-a8, 35 Rc1-c7 Bd7-c8, 36 Rb7xa7+ Ka8-b8, 37 Na3-b5 and mates in three. You should work this out on your own.

33 ...	Rd8-c8
34 Rc7-b7+	Kb8-a8
35 Rb7xd7!	Rc8xc1
36 Na3xb5	....

In conjunction with his advanced and soon to be passed Pawn and his active Knight and King, White's rook on the seventh rank is more than enough compensation for the Exchange. Now there is only one defense to White's threat of 37 Rd7xa7+ Ka8-b8, 38 Ra7-b7+ Kb8-c8 (or 38 ... Kb8-a8 39 Nb5-c7 mate), 39 Nb5-a7+ Kc8-d8, 40 Rb7-b8+, and so on.

36	Rh8-c8
37 Rd7xg7	h7-h6

38 Rg7xa7+	Ka8-b8
39 Ra7-b7+	Kb8-a8
40 Rb7-a7+	Ka8-b8
41 Ra7-b7+	Kb8-a8
42 g3-g4	....

White's plan is simple. A general advance of his kingside Pawn majority should net some passed Pawns. Black's Rooks are tied down to the defense. Rather than wait passively, Black attempts to break the bind.

42	e6-c5
43 d4-d5	Rc1-c5
44 Rb7-a7+	Ka8-b8
45 Ra7-b7+	Kb8-a8
46 Rb7xb6	Rc8-b8
47 Rb6xb8+	Ka8xb8
48 a6-a7+	Kb8-b7
49 Nb5-d6+	Kb7xa7
50 Nd6-e8	Ka7-b6
51 Ne8xf6	....

Figure 10-34   White is winning.

White has established a winning material advantage, and the rest is technique.

| 51 .... | Rc5-c3+ |
| 52 Ke3-f2 | Rc3-c7 |

53 h2-h4	Rc7-f7
54 Nf6-h5	Kb6-c7
55 g4-g5	h6xg5
56 h4xg5	Rf7-h7
57 Nh5-f6	Rh7-h2+
58 Kf2-g3	Rh2-h1
59 Kg3-g2	Rh1-h8
60 g5-g6	Resigns

On 60 ... Rh8-h6, 61 g6-g7 Rh6-g6+, 62 Kg2-f2 Rg6xg7, 63 Nf6-e8+ wins the Rook.

The off-side majority

The off-side majority, sometimes called the queenside majority since both players usually castle on the kingside, refers to a Pawn majority that is on the opposite side of the board from the two Kings. A more precise definition of an off-side majority is a Pawn majority (or passed Pawn) that is the farthest from the largest group of Pawns. For instance, in a position where one player has a 2:1 majority and the other a 4:3 majority, the 2:1 majority is considered off-side and constitutes an advantage. In the endgame, it is often a decisive advantage.

Let's examine the principles involved by first looking at a pure Pawn ending. In Figure 10-35, Black has a passed e-pawn, but White can create a passed Pawn on the h-file. White's passed Pawn will be farthest from the bulk of the Pawns (and away from the soon to be centralized Kings) and is thus the off-side majority. The winning

Figure 10-35   Lasker-Allies (Moscow, 1899).

procedure is identical to that of the decoy principle (Chapter 8):
Once the passed Pawn is created, White will create a winning
material advantage on the other side of the board. This will be
possible, since the Black King will have to run down the passer.

1	h2-h4	a7-a5
2	g2-g4	a5-a4
3	Kg1-f2	a4-a3
4	Kf2-e3	Kf7-e6
5	Ke3-e4	Ke6-f6

Both sides have centralized their Kings. White's King is blockading
the passed e-pawn, so the Pawn cannot go very far. But the position
is hopeless for Black, since his King will be forced off-side by White's
outside passed Pawn.

6	c3-c4	b7-b6
7	c2-c3	Kf6-e6
8	h4-h5	g6xh5
9	g4xh5	Ke6-f6
10	h5-h6	Kf6-g6
11	Ke4xe5	Kg6xh6
12	Ke5-d6	Resigns

White wins Black's Pawns and promotes his own.

Now let's look at a more complicated example. From Figure
10-36, White manages under pressure to maintain material equality,
but loses in the classic manner to the off-side majority.

Figure 10-36   Marshall-Tarrasch
(Nuremberg, 1905).

1 c3xd4	c5xb4!
2 d4xe5	Ke7-e6
3 d3-d4	b4xa3
4 Kd2-c3	a3-a2

Black's pawn majority is farthest from the center and from the mass of kingside Pawns. It turns out that White cannot prevent the exchange of his passed pawns for Black's, leaving the Black King nearer the remaining Pawns.

5 g2-g4	g6-g5
6 Kc3-d3	b5-b4
7 Kd3-c4	b4-b3+
8 Kc4xb3	....

If 8 Kc4-c3 Ra4xd4!, 9 Kc3xd4 b3-b2 wins.

8	Ra4xd4
9 Ra1xa2	Rd4xe4
10 Ra2-a6	Re4-e3+
11 Kb3-c2	Re3xh3
12 Ra6xb6+	Ke6xe5
13 Rb6-b4	Rh3-e3
14 Kc2-d2	Re3-e4

White resigned because of 15 Rb4-b7 Ke5-f4! (keeping the White King cut off with the Black Rook), 16 Rb7xh7 Kf4xg4, and Black has reached a well-known winning position.

Figure 10-37   Naegeli-Alekhine (Zurich, 1934).

One must be careful to differentiate between a healthy, mobile Pawn majority and a crippled one. For instance, in Figure 10-37, White clearly has the off-side majority, away from the largest cluster of Pawns, but is quite lost since he cannot mobilize them. Black's one Pawn on the queenside holds White's two, making Black in effect a Pawn ahead. Play continues:

1	Kf6-e5
2 Rb3-e3	f7-f5

Black proceeds to advance his kingside majority as though he were a Pawn ahead. White can only defend passively, since there is no way to use his extra queenside Pawn.

3 h2-h4	Ke5-d4
4 Re3-b3	h7-h6
5 Rb3-e3	....

If 5 Rb3-b1 to activate the Rook, then 5 ... Rc4-c3, 6 Rb1-a1 e4-e3+, 7 f2xe3+ Rc3xe3, and Black gobbles up the kingside Pawns.

5	g6-g5
6 h4xg5	h6xg5
7 Re3-b3	Rc4-c8!

Black finds a more active Rook position on the h-file.

8 Rb3-e3	Rc8-h8
9 Re3-e2	f5-f4
10 g3xf4	g5xf4

Compare 10-38 to the previous one. Black has methodically advanced his kingside majority and kept his Rook and King very active. He now threatens to make a passed Pawn to which there is no adequate defense.

11 Kd2-c2	Rh8-h2
12 Kc2-b3	....

White finally is in a position to create a passed Pawn, but Black cautiously squelches that threat before proceeding.

Figure 10-38   After 10 ... g5xf4, White is helpless.

12	Rh2-h3+
13 Kb3-b2	Rh3-d3

This cuts off the White King from getting back to stop the imminent passed Pawn.

14 Re2-c2	f4-f3
15 Kb2-c1	e4-e3
16 f2xe3+	Kd4xe3

White resigns. He must give up his Rook to stop the Pawn's promotion after 17 Rc2-c8 f3-f2, 18 Rc8-e8+ Ke3-f3 18 Kcl-c2 (18 Re8-f8+ Kf3-e2 19 Rf8-e8+ Rd3-e3) Rd3-e3.

Using the King

In the opening and middle game, the King must be protected with great care or it might become exposed to a direct attack. But when many pieces have been exchanged and the endgame is reached, the requirements of the position changes. Then one's King must be brought forward, usually into the center, in order to take part in the action. In the endgame, the King must be thought of as an active piece just like any other. Failure to understand this principle can be the difference between winning and losing. Let's look at some examples.

Figure 10-39 finds White with a small advantage. His pieces

Figure 10-39 Capablanca-Kostics (Havana, 1919).

are more active, and he has a space advantage on the kingside derived from the advanced f-pawn. True, White has doubled and isolated Pawns, but the strength of the front f-pawn outweighs this weakness. Yet the major advantage White has is his King! It can be brought into play easily, whereas Black's King is difficult to activate. Watch how Capablanca, perhaps the greatest endgame player of all time, brings home the point.

$$1 \ldots \ldots \qquad \text{Be8-d7}$$

The immediate attempt to liquidate the pressure exerted by the f5 Pawn, 1 ... g7-g6, fails to 2 Bh2-f4!, which forces 2 ... g6-g5. Black is then left with a further weakness at f6. Still, this might have been preferable to the game continuation because it might then have been more difficult to penetrate with the White King.

2 Bd5-e4	Ra3-a6
3 Re3-d3	Bd7-c6
4 Be4xc6	Ra6xc6
5 Kg1-g2	....

The exchange of light-squared Bishops has only aided White. Black's remaining Bishop is severely restricted by his own Pawns, and now White's King is free to penetrate on the light squares.

5	Rc6-a6
6 Kg2-f3	Ra6-a2
7 Bh2-g3	Kf8-e8

Note how Black's King cannot get into the game, since it is hemmed in by the f5 Pawn and the White Rook. Therefore, Black should have tried 7 ... Ra2-a7, followed by 8 ... Kf8-f7 and 9 ... g7-g6.

8 Bg3-f4	Ra2-a3
9 Bf4-e3	Ra3-a1
10 Kf3-g4	Ra1-a7
11 Kg4-h5	Ke8-f7

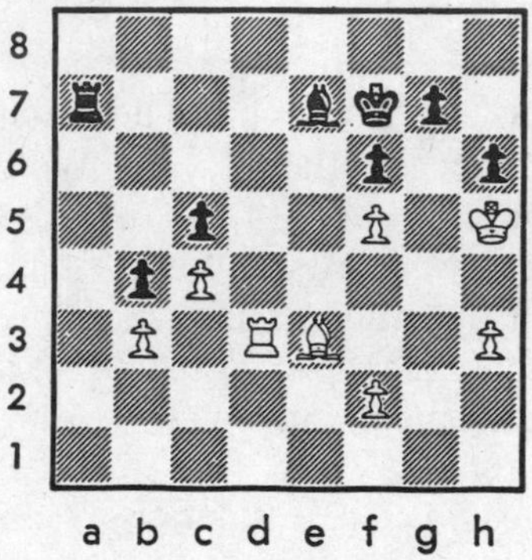

Figure 10-40   White maneuvers for a breakthrough.

White has placed all of his pieces on their optimum squares and now only needs to find a way to break through. If his King can get into g6, the game will be over.

12 Rd3-d5	Ra7-a3
13 Rd5-d7	Kf7-e8

White would win a piece on 13 ... Ra3xb3, 14 Be3xc5.

14 Rd7-d3	Ke8-f7
15 h3-h4	Ra3-a7
16 Rd3-d5	Ra7-a5

After 16 ... Ra7-c7, 17 f2-f3! Rc7-c6, 18 Rd5 d7 (7th rank!) Kf7-e8, 19 Rd7-a7 Ke8-f7, 20 Be3-f4! (tieing the Black Rook to the 6th rank, or else Bf4-d6 wins) Rc6-b6, 21 Ra7-c7 Rb6-a6, 22 Bf4-e3 wins.

17 Rd5-d7	Kf8-e8
18 Rd7-d3	Ke8-f7
19 Rd3-d5!	....

If now 19 ... Be7-f8, 20 Rd5-d7+ Bf8-e7, 21 Rd7-c7, and Black must move his King and allow Kh5-g6.

19	Ra5-a3
20 Be3xc5	Be7xc5
21 Rd4xc5	Ra3xb3
22 Rc5-c7+	Kf7-f8
23 Kh5-g6	....

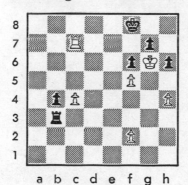

Figure 10-41   The entrance of the King is decisive.

The triumph of the active King—Black is helpless. The remainder of the game, which will reward close study, is given without notes.

23	Rb3-f3
24 Rc7-f7+	Kf8-e8
25 Rf7xg7	Rf3-f4
26 h4-h5	Rf4xc4
27 Kg6xh6	Ke8-f8

28 Rg7-b7	Rc4-g4
29 f2-f3	Rg4-g5
30 Rb7xb4	Kf8-f7
31 Rb4-g4	Rg5xf5
32 f3-f4	Rf5-a5
33 Rg4-g7+	Kf7-f8
34 Rg7-b7	f6-f5
35 Kh6-g6	Ra5-a6+
36 Kg6xf5	Ra6-a5+
37 Kf5-g4	Ra5-a6
38 Kg4-g5	Ra6-c6
39 f4-f5	Kf8-g8
40 f5-f6	Rc6-c1
41 Rb7-g7+	Kg8-f8
42 h5-h6	Resigns

III
THE BATTLE

chapter eleven
ILLUSTRATIVE GAMES

Janowski—Marshall
(Biarritz, 1912)

1	e2-e4	e7-e5
2	Ng1-f3	Ng8-f6
3	Nf3xe5	d7-d6

Well known is the trap 3 ... Nf6xe4? 4 Qd1-e2 Ne4-f6??, 5 Ne5-c6+, winning the Queen. This is an extreme example of the calamity that can befall you on the open e-file if you are not careful.

4	Ne5-f3	Nf6xe4
5	d2-d4	d6-d5
6	Bf1-d3	Bf8-d6
7	c2-c4	....

It is better to castle first before starting operations to undermine the obtrusive Black Knight on e4.

7	....	0-0
8	c4xd5	....

Best is 8 0-0. White must surely have regretted this hasty Pawn capture.

8 .... Bd6-b4+

Now if 9 Nb1-d2 Ne4xd2, then 10 Bc1xd2 Rf8-e8+ leaves Black with a clear advantage (better development and pressure on the d-pawn), so White decides to forego castling in the hope of gaining a superiority in the center.

9 Ke1-f1 Qd8xd5
10 Qd1-c2 Rf8-e8
11 Nb1-c3 ....

White expects 11 ... Bb4xc3, 12 b2xc3 with some central Pawns to show for his uncastled King. But Black has a surprise up his sleeve.

11 .... Ne4xc3
12 b2xc3 ....

Figure 11-1   Black to move.

You may wish to study the diagrammed position before looking at Black's next move.

12 .... Qd5xf3!

If now 13 g2xf3 Bc8-h3+, 14 Kf1-g1 Re8-e1 mate!; such is the power of active pieces against an exposed King. But Black has seen much more, as the sequel will show.

13 c3xb4 ....

Best was 13 h2-h3! (threatening to take the Queen) Qf3-d5, 14 c3xb4 Qd5xd4, 15 Bc1-b2 Qd4xb4, 16 Bd3xh7+Kg8-h8, 17 Bh7-d3, with active pieces for the lost Pawn.

13 .... **Nb8-c6**

Development with tempo.

14 Bc1-b2 ....

This move is now an error. Correct was 14 h2-h3 or 14 Bc1-d2. Apparently the back rank is now defended, and White is ready to take the Queen, or so he thinks.

14 .... **Nc6xb4!**

A fine piece sacrifice.

15 Bd3xh7+	**Kg8-h8**
16 g2xf3	**Nb4xc2**
17 Bh7xc2	**Bc8-h3+**
18 Kf1-g1	**Re8-e2**

Occupying the seventh rank with tempo.

19 Ra1-c1 **Ra8-e8**

Black is now threatening 20 ... Re2-e1+ mating, as well as 20 ... Re2xc2. White's move is forced.

20 Bb2-c3 **Re8-e3!!**

Figure 11-2   After 20 Bb2-c3, White is
in a mating net.

Also winning was 20 . . . Re2xc2! 21 Rc1xc2 Re8-e6, and there is no
defense to . . . Re6-g6.

After the text, 21 f2xe3 loses to Re2-g2+, 22 Kg1-f1 Rg2xc2+,
followed by 23 . . . Rc2xc1+ and 24 . . . Rc1xh1, demonstrating the
power of the discovered check.

21	Bc3-b4	Re3xf3
22	Bc2-d1	Rf3-f6

And White resigns as 23 Bd1xe2 Rf6-g6+ leads to mate.

Winawer-Steinitz
(Nuremberg, 1896)

1	e2-e4	e7-e5
2	d2-d4	e5xd4
3	Qd1xd4	Nb8-c6

Black develops a piece with tempo, attacking White's Queen. This is
precisely the reason that 2 d2-d4 is rarely played except as in the
Danish Gambit with 3 c2-c3 (see Figure 8-17).

4	Qd4-e3	Ng8-f6
5	Nb1-c3	Bf8-b4
6	Bc1-d2	0-0
7	0-0-0	Rf8-e8

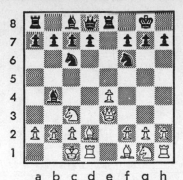

Figure 11-3   Development is top priority.

White castled queenside because he had developed that side first. It is important to get the King out of the center quickly when the center is as open as it is here.

Black's last move activates his Rook on the half-open e-file and threatens to win a Pawn by 8 . . . Bb4xc3, 9 Bd2xc3 Nf6xe4. If White defends with 8 f2-f3 or 8 Bf1-d3, Black gets the advantage with 8 . . . d7-d5, utilizing the pin of the White e-pawn to obtain the initiative. Therefore, White decides to sacrifice the Pawn and jump ahead in development.

8 Bf1-c4	**Bb4xc3**

It would have been better to forego the win of the Pawn and complete development with 8 . . . d7-d6 followed by Bc8-e6.

9 Bd2xc3	**Nf6xe4**
10 Qe3-f4	**Ne4-f6**
11 Ng1-f3	**d7-d6**
12 Nf3-g5	**Bc8-e6**
13 Bc4-d3	**. . . .**

White, of course, refrains from exchanging off his aggressive pieces, since that would blunt the attack.

13	**h7-h6**
14 h2-h4!	**. . . .**

Figure 11-4   White is poised for the attack.

You have seen this idea before (Figure 9-44). White looks for ways to bring more pieces into the attack, in this case, the Rooks. If now 14 ... h6xg5, 15 h4xg5 Nf6-d5, 16 Qf4-h4 (threatening mate) Kg8-f8, 17 Bc3xg7+! Kf8-e7 (if Black captures the Bishop, it's mate in two), 18 Bd3-c4 (threatening to win the Knight on d5 as well as 19 Bc4xd5 Be6xd5, 20 Bg7-f6+, winning the Queen) Re8-g8, 19 Qh4-h6! with a strong attack for the material sacrificed.

14 ....   Nf6-d5?

This move is not logical, because it removes a vital defender from the threatened sector. Also bad would be 14 ... Be6xa2, since after 15 b2-b3, the Bishop is buried alive. But after a move such as 14 ... d6-d5, controlling the central squares and threatening to gain space with d5-d4, it is not clear how White can strengthen the attack.

15 Bd3-h7+   Kg8-h8
16 Rd1xd5!   Be6xd5
17 Bh7-e4!   ....

Figure 11-5   A stunning blow!

In addition to the Bishop on d5, White threatens 18 Ng5xf7 Bd5xf7, 19 Qf4xh6+, leading to mate as the g-pawn is pinned. Black's best defense is to give back the Exchange with 17 ... Re8xe4, 18 Ng5xe4 (on 18 Ng5xf7+ Kh8-g8!) Nc6-e5.

It is interesting to observe how the Rook on h1 is participating in the attack, because if 17 ... h6xg5, 18 h4xg5+ Kh8-g8, 19 g5-g6!! wins at once: (a) 19 ... Re8xe4 20 Rh1-h8+!! Kg8xh8, 21 Qf4-h6+ and mate on g7; or (b) 19 ... Re8-e5 (or Nc6-e5), 20 Be4xd5, and Black cannot meet all of White's threats.

The use of the powerful White Bishops in these variations is exemplary. The sacrifice of the Exchange on move 16 in the game can be understood by comparing the activity of the White Bishop on

Figure 11-6   After 19 g5-g6!! (analysis)

c3 to the Black Rook on a8. This game represents a clear case of a
localized material advantage, if there ever was one.

17	f7-f6
18 Be4xd5	f6xg5
19 h4xg5	Nc6-e5
20 g5-g6!	Resigns

There is no answer to 21 Rh1xh6 (that Rook again) g7xh6, 22 Qf4xh6
mate.

Pillsbury—Lasker
(Cambridge Springs, 1904)

1 d2-d4	d7-d5
2 c2-c4	e7-e6
3 Nb1-c3	Ng8-f6
4 Ng1-f3	c7-c5
5 Bc1-g5	c5xd4
6 Qd1xd4	Nb8-c6
7 Bg5xf6	g7xf6

Black must play this move, because 7 . . . Nc6xd4, 8 Bf6xd8 Nd4-c2+,
9 Ke1-d2 Nc2xa1, 10 Bd8-h4 will leave Black behind in material
when the trapped Knight on a1 is eventually captured. If Black plays
7 . . . Qd8xf6, he loses a Pawn to 8 Qd4xf6 g7xf6, 9 c4xd5.

| 8 Qd4-h4 | d5xc4 |
| 9 Ra1-d1 | . . . . |

The White Rook takes the d-file without loss of time as it attacks the
Black Queen.

| 9 . . . . | Bc8-d7 |
| 10 e2-e3 | . . . . |

White now plans to finish his kingside development with Bf1xc4 and
0-0. Black tries to disrupt this plan.

| 10 . . . . | Nc6-e5 |
| 11 Nf3xe5 | f6xe5 |

12	Qh4xc4	Qd8-b6
13	Bf1-e2!	....

Figure 11-7   White gambits the b-pawn.

White offers the b-pawn, but the offer should be declined, because Black will lose valuable time capturing it. The net result of the opening has left Black with a shattered Pawn structure and therefore no safe place to put his King.

13	....	Qb6xb2?
14	0-0	Ra8-c8
15	Qc4-d3	Rc8-c7

The White threat on d7 precluded Black from capturing on c3.

16	Nc3-e4	Bf8-e7
17	Ne4-d6+	Ke8-f8

Black must forego castling. No better is 17 ... Be7xd6, 18 Qd3xd6 Qb2-b6 (not 18 ... Qb2xe2, 19 Qd6xc7 or 18 ... Qb2-c3, 19 Be2-b5!), 19 Qd6xe5.

18	Nd6-c4	Qb2-b5

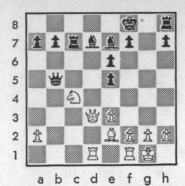

Figure 11-8   How can White activate more
pieces?

White has a nice position for the Pawn, but must quickly find a way
to activate his remaining pieces before Black can consolidate his
exposed King.

        19 f2-f4   ....

Black should now probably play 19 ... e5-e4, returning the Pawn,
but keeping the f-file closed.

        19 ....   e5xf4
        20 Qd3-d4!   f7-f6

Black is forced to further weaken his King, since protecting the Rook
by Rh8-g8 loses to 21 Qd4xf4, with a double attack on c7 and f7.

        21 Qd4xf4   Qb5-c5
        22 Nc4-e5!   ....

White makes use of the pin of the f-pawn (22 ... Qc5xe5??, 23
Qf4xe5) to bring up more attacking units.

        22 ....   Bd7-e8
        23 Ne5-g4   f6-f5
        24 Qf4-h6+   Kf8-f7
        25 Be2-c4!   ....

Figure 11-9   The final piece enters the attack.

The White Bishop enters the fray by taking advantage of the potential fork on e5 (if 25 ... Qc5xc4, 26 Ng4-e5+ wins the Queen). Now every White piece is converging on the Black King, and it is no wonder that Black's scattered forces are helpless.

25	Rc7-c6
26 Rf1xf5+	Qc5xf5
27 Rd1-f1	Qf5-xf1+
28 Kg1xf1	....

The White Bishop on c4 is still immune from capture.

28	Be8-d7
29 Qh6-h5+	Kf7-g8
30 Ng4-e5	Resigns

White is threatening 31 Qf7 mate as well as several pieces. If 30 ... Kg8-g7, 31 Qh5-f7+ Kg7-h6, 32 Qf7xe7, and further resistance is hopeless.

Nimzovich—Capablanca
(New York, 1927)

1 e2-e4	c7-c6
2 d2-d4	d7-d5
3 e4-e5	....

The usual move is 3 Nb1-c3. The text keeps the center closed and gives White a space advantage with the advanced Pawn on e5. But there is no pressure on Black's position, and he can develop quite easily.

                3 ....   Bc8-f5

Note that this is played *before* e7-e6, since that would shut in the light-squared Bishop *behind* the Pawns.

                4 Bf1-d3   Bf5xd3
                5 Qd1xd3   e7-e6
                6 Nb1-c3   Qd8-b6

Usually, it is best not to bring out the Queen too early. Here it is a good move, since the center is closed and the Queen cannot be easily harrassed by White's pieces. Black prepares c6-c5 to activate the queenside.

                7 Ng1-e2   c6-c5
                8 d4xc5   Bf8xc5
                9 0-0   Ng8-e7
               10 Nc3-a4   Qb6-c6
               11 Na4xc5   Qc6xc5
               12 Bc1-e3   Qc5-c7
               13 f2-f4   Ne7-f5

Let's evaluate the position in Figure 11-10. White still has a space advantage on the kingside (the Pawn at e5 cramps Black), but finds it difficult to attack there as Black has a fine blockade of the f5 square. White can control f5 and attack with the move g2-g4, but this leaves his own King permanently weakened with no Pawn shelter.

Black will clearly operate on the queenside, attempting to make something of his control of the c-file. The only question that remains is: What will Black do with his King? Since the center is rather blocked, Black prefers to wait with that decision. Indeed, if the major action is going to take place on the wings, the King is actually safer in the center.

Figure 11-10   Where will Black put his King?

14 c2-c3	Nb8-c6
15 Ra1-d1	g7-g6
16 g2-g4	....

Black's last move created holes at f6 and h6, but how is White to occupy them? In any case, White decides that he can no longer tolerate the Knight on f5 and weakens his own King.

16	Nf5xe3
17 Qd3xe3	h7-h5!

White is now forced to lock up the kingside, because if 18 h2-h3 h5xg4, 19 h3xg4 0-0-0!, Black will attack by doubling Rooks on the h-file.

18 g4-g5	0-0!

Black connects his Rooks and puts his King into safety. White has no way to open the kingside or to exploit the holes at f6 and h6. There are also holes in the White position (g4, f5, e4).

19 Ne2-d4	Qc7-b6
20 Rf1-f2	Rf8-c8
21 a2-a3	....

Now there is a hole at b3 as well!

21	Rc8-c7
22 Rd1-d3	Nc6-a5
23 Rf2-e2	Ra8-e8!

White was threatening 24 f4-f5 e6xf5 (g6xf5, g5-g6!), 25 e5-e6, breaking into Black's position with a Pawn sacrifice. The text move prevents this.

24 Kg1-g2	Na5-c6
25 Re2-d2	Re8-c8

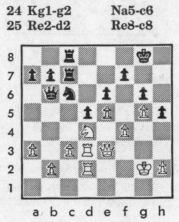

Figure 11-11   The pressure on the c-file mounts.

White has no play and must wait for Black to show his hand. Best is now 26 Nd4xc6, since the Black Knight now finds his way to one of White's holes.

26 Rd2-e2	Nc6-e7!
27 Re2-d2	Rc7-c4
28 Qe3-h3	Kg8-g7
29 Rd2-f2	a7-a5
30 Rf2-e2	Ne7-f5!

Figure 11-12   Black exchanges off White's best piece.

If now 31 Nd4xf5+ g6xf5!, 32 Qh3xh5 Rc8-h8, 33 Qh5-f3 Rh8-h4, and Black breaks through to the "loose" White King. But White cannot let Black capture on d4, since the Pawn that ends up there would be pitifully weak.

31	Nd4xf5+	g6xf5
32	Qh3-f3	Kg7-g6
33	Re2-d2	Rc4-e4!

Finally, one of White's holes is occupied.

34	Rd3-d4	Rc8-c4
35	Qf3-f2	Qb6-b5
36	Kg2-g3	Rc4xd4
37	c3xd4	....

This is forced because 37 Rd2xd4 Re4-e2 loses at once. Now Black inches his way in, and White is soon out of safe moves! The weak Pawns on d4 and f4 and the many holes, coupled with White's exposed King, are fatal.

37	....	Qb5-c4
38	Kg3-g2	b7-b5
39	Kg2-g1	b5-b4

40 a3xb4	a5xb4
41 Kg1-g2	Qc4-c1!

White now cannot move his Queen or Rook. And if he does nothing, Black might invade c2 with the aid of the advanced b-Pawn, for example, 42 h2-h3 b4-b3, 43 Kg2-h2 Re4-e1, 44 Kh2-g2 Qc1-b1, 45 Rd2-e2 Re1-c1, followed by Rc1-c2.

42 Kg2-g3	Qc1-h1!
43 Rd2-d3	Re4-e1
44 Rd3-f3	Re1-d1
45 b2-b3	Rd1-c1!

Figure 11-13   The encirclement is complete.

The only moves White has left lose immediately, as a few sample variations will show. This situation has a special name: White is said to be in **zugzwang,** a German word for compulsion to move. If 46 h2-h3 Rc1-g1+, 47 Kg3-h4 Rg1-g4 mate! If 46 Kg3-h4 Rc1-c2, 47 Qf2xc2 Qh1xf3, 48 h2-h3 Qf3xf4 mate. You might try to work out the forced wins for Black after the other possible White moves.

46 Rf3-e3	Rc1-f1
47 Resigns	

If 47 Qf2-e2 Qh1-g1+, 48 Kg3-h3 Rf1-f2, and Black mates next.

GLOSSARY

advanced Pawn any Pawn that crosses the fourth rank of either player; such a Pawn confers a space advantage on the player who possesses it.

algebraic notation the internationally recognized way of recording the moves of a chess game.

Bishop a minor piece that moves diagonally and has an approximate value of three units.

blunder a move that is a serious mistake.

capture moving your own piece or Pawn to a square occupied by an opponent's and removing the other from the board.

castling a special move whereby the King, standing on its original square, moves two squares to the right or left and the corresponding Rook is placed adjacent to the King on the opposite side. This move is subject to certain restrictions.

center strictly speaking, the four most central squares on the chess board—e4, e5, d4, d5; the most important area of the board.

check the word called out when one attacks the opponent's King; a King under attack is said to be in check and must get out of check at once.

checkmate the ultimate object of the game, when a King is in check but has no legal moves; often called simply "mate."

chessboard the field of battle in chess consisting of 64 alternating light and dark squares.

combination a series of moves, usually involving a sacrifice, whose ultimate aim is winning material or checkmate.

compensation one type of advantage that counterbalances a disadvantage; usually refers to a strategic advantage that offsets a material disadvantage.

development bringing out one's pieces off the back rank and into play; the major goal of the opening.

discovered attack the uncovering of an attack by one piece; the attack results from moving a second piece.

discovered check a type of discovered attack where the piece that is uncovered gives check.

double check a discovered check where two pieces give check simultaneously.

doubled Pawns two Pawns of the same color on the same file.

draw the result of a chess game where there is no winner.

endgame the stage of the game played with a greatly reduced number of pieces and Pawns; the stage of the game when the Kings can become active.

en passant a special move that is allowed a Pawn which stands on its own fifth rank.

en prise a term for a piece or Pawn which is attacked but undefended.

exchange a sequence of moves where each player captures some of the opponent's units.

Exchange a special term for the trading of a Rook for a minor piece; winning a Rook for a minor piece is called "winning the Exchange."

file the vertical rows on the chessboard; in algebraic notation the a-file, b-file, and so on.

forced move chess jargon for a move which, if not made, would lead to an immediately lost position.

fork a move which attacks two units simultaneously.

gambit the sacrificing of material for some other advantage; usually occurs in the opening where a Pawn or more is given up in exchange for an advantage in development (time).

half-open file a file on which only one player has a Pawn; the other player has a half-open file.

hole a square of strategic value which can no longer be defended by an opponent's Pawn.

initiative attacking play; the player who is launching the threats is said to "have the initiative."

isolated Pawn a Pawn whose two adjacent files contain no Pawn of the same color.

J'adoube French for "I adjust"; the phrase said aloud before adjusting any pieces on the board.

King the ultimate target in a chess game; it moves one square at a time in any direction.

kingside refers to the half of the board from the e-file to the h-file.

Knight a minor piece which moves in an L-shaped manner and has an approximate value of three units.

lever opposite color Pawns that are in position to capture one another; for example, a White Pawn on e4 and a Black Pawn on d5.

major pieces the Rooks and Queens.

mate short for checkmate.

material forces; pieces and Pawns; if one player has pieces of greater value than the opponent, he or she has a material advantage.

mating net when a player's King is surrounded by the enemy, so that he is checkmated or soon will be.

middle game the stage of the game that occurs after most of the pieces are developed; after the opening, but before the endgame.

minor pieces the Bishops and Knights.

notation a method of recording the moves of a game.

open file a file on which neither player has any Pawns.

opening the stage of the game where each player's pieces are developed; often includes castling.

overworked piece a piece that has too many defensive tasks.

passed Pawn a Pawn which can advance to promotion without being hindered by an opponent's Pawn.

Pawn the footsoldiers of a chess game, each with a value of one unit; they move only directly forward and capture diagonally.

Pawn storm an attacking phalanx where an entire wing of Pawns is advanced on the enemy's castled King.

perpetual check a position in which one player can demonstrate that he or she can check continuously; one type of draw.

piece generally refers to all forces except the Pawns; thus, one's army consists of pieces and Pawns.

pin a tactical motif where one piece limits the mobility of an opponent's piece.

promotion the replacing of a Pawn by a Queen, Rook, Bishop, or Knight, when it reaches the eighth rank.

Queen a major piece that may move horizontally, vertically, or diagonally and is valued at approximately nine units; the most valuable piece on the board.

queening promotion of a Pawn to a Queen.

queenside refers to the half of the board from the d-file to the a-file.

rank the horizontal rows on the chessboard; in algebraic notation, they are numbered 1 to 8 from White's side.

Rook a major piece which moves horizontally or vertically and has a value of approximately five units.

sacrifice voluntarily giving up material for some other advantage.

seventh rank usually considered the most powerful position for a Rook; Black's seventh rank is White's second rank.

smothered mate a special type of checkmate, delivered by a Knight, where the King's escape is blocked by its own pieces and Pawns.

stalemate a type of draw, when one player has no legal move on the entire board, but is not in check.

strategy plans or goals in a chess game; often refers to maneuvering.

tactics the actual moves that carry out one's strategy; often refers to special motifs such as pins, discovered checks, forks, and so on.

target a square or object of attack.

tempo literally, time; generally refers to one move in a game; wasting a move is called "losing a tempo."

thematic a move or idea which follows a common chess strategy.

time generally refers to development of the pieces; one who has lost time is usually behind in development.

touch move the formal rule which says that if you touch one of your pieces you must move it if it is legally possible.

zugzwang German for "compulsion to move"; a situation, usually occurring in the endgame, in which every move worsens the position or loses at once.

INDEX